S0-ASN-898

HOW DO WE KNOW
WHAT WE KNOW?

This is the problem that epistemology deals
with—and upon the solution of this problem
every other aspect of philosophy must rest. For
until we know *how* we know, we cannot be
certain of *what* we know. And if we cannot know
anything with certainty, our capacity to reason,
to choose and to act is subverted at the root.

In a world poisoned by the doctrines of
irrationalism, a world afflicted by a sense
of helplessness and hopelessness,
INTRODUCTION TO OBJECTIVIST
EPISTEMOLOGY serves as an invaluable
antidote. Here is the foundation of a system of
thought—and a view of man's potential—that
returns us from a shadowland of intellectual
paralysis and despair to the real world of
individual strength and the efficacious mind.

INTRODUCTION TO OBJECTIVIST EPISTEMOLOGY

by

Ayn Rand

With an Additional Essay by Leonard Peikoff

A MENTOR BOOK

NEW AMERICAN LIBRARY

TIMES MIRROR

New York and Scarborough, Ontario
The New English Library Limited, London

Introduction to Objectivist Epistemology: Copyright © 1966, 1967,
by The Objectivist, Inc.

First published in *The Objectivist* July 1966–February 1967
Library of Congress Catalog Card Number: 67-22335

The Analytic-Synthetic Dichotomy: © Copyright 1967 by The
Objectivist, Inc.

Originally appeared, in five parts in the May, June, July,
August and September, 1967, issues of *The Objectivist*

Library of Congress Catalog Card Number: 78-71454

 MENTOR TRADEMARK REG. U.S. PAT. OFF. AND FOREIGN COUNTRIES
REGISTERED TRADEMARK—MARCA REGISTRADA
HECHO EN CHICAGO, U.S.A.

SIGNET, SIGNET CLASSICS, MENTOR, PLUME, MERIDIAN AND NAL
Books are published *in the United States* by
The New American Library, Inc.,
1633 Broadway, New York, New York 10019;
in Canada by The New American Library of Canada Limited,
81 Mack Avenue, Scarborough, Ontario M1L 1M8;
in the United Kingdom by The New English Library Limited,
Barnard's Inn, Holborn, London EC1N 2JR, England

First Mentor Printing, April, 1979

4   5   6   7   8   9   10   11   12

PRINTED IN THE UNITED STATES OF AMERICA

Contents

INTRODUCTION TO
OBJECTIVIST EPISTEMOLOGY

by

Ayn Rand

Foreword

(This work was first published in
The Objectivist July 1966–February 1967.)

This series of articles is presented "by popular demand." We have had so many requests for information on Objectivist epistemology that I decided to put on record a summary of one of its cardinal elements—the Objectivist theory of concepts. These articles may be regarded as a preview of my future book on Objectivism, and are offered here for the guidance of philosophy students.

The issue of concepts (known as "the problem of universals") is philosophy's central issue. Since man's knowledge is gained and held in conceptual form, the validity of man's knowledge depends on the validity of concepts. But concepts are abstractions or universals, and everything that man perceives is particular, concrete. What is the relationship between abstractions and concretes? To what precisely do concepts refer in reality? Do they refer to something real, something that exists—or are they merely inventions of man's mind, arbitrary constructs or loose approximations that cannot claim to represent knowledge?

"All knowledge is in terms of concepts. If these concepts correspond to something that is to be found in reality they are real and man's knowledge has a foundation in fact; if they do not correspond to anything in reality they are not real and man's knowledge is of mere figments of his own imagination." (Edward C. Moore, *American Pragmatism: Peirce, James, & Dewey*, New York: Columbia University Press, 1961, p. 27.)

To exemplify the issue as it is usually presented: When we refer to three persons as "men," what do we designate by that term? The three persons are three individuals who differ in every particular respect and may not possess a single *identical* characteristic (not even their fingerprints). If you list all their particular characteristics, you will not find one representing "manness." Where is the "manness" in men? What, in reality, corresponds to the concept "man" in our mind?

In the history of philosophy, there are, essentially, four schools of thought on this issue:

1. The "extreme realists" or Platonists, who hold that abstractions exist as real entities or archetypes in another dimension of reality and that the concretes we perceive are merely their imperfect reflections, but the concretes evoke the abstractions in our mind. (According to Plato, they do so by evoking the memory of the archetypes which we had known, before birth, in that other dimension.)

2. The "moderate realists," whose ancestor (unfortunately) is Aristotle, who hold that abstractions exist in reality, but they exist only *in* concretes, in the form of metaphysical *essences,* and that our concepts refer to these essences.

3. The "nominalists," who hold that all our ideas are only images of concretes, and that ab-

stractions are merely "names" which we give to arbitrary groupings of concretes on the basis of vague resemblances.

4. The "conceptualists," who share the nominalists' view that abstractions have no actual basis in reality, but who hold that concepts exist in our minds as some sort of ideas, not as images.

(There is also the extreme nominalist position, the modern one, which consists of declaring that the problem is a meaningless issue, that "reality" is a meaningless term, that we can never know whether our concepts correspond to anything or not, that our knowledge consists of words—and that words are an arbitrary social convention.)

If, in the light of such "solutions," the problem might appear to be esoteric, let me remind you that the fate of human societies, of knowledge, of science, of progress and of every human life, depends on it. What is at stake here is the cognitive efficacy of man's mind.

As I wrote in *For the New Intellectual:* "To negate man's mind, it is the *conceptual* level of his consciousness that has to be invalidated. Under all the tortuous complexities, contradictions, equivocations, rationalizations of the post-Renaissance philosophy—the one consistent line, the fundamental that explains the rest, is: *a concerted attack on man's conceptual faculty.* Most philosophers did not intend to invalidate conceptual knowledge, but its defenders did more to destroy it than did its enemies. They were unable to offer a solution to the 'problem of universals,' that is: to define the nature and source of abstractions, to determine the relationship of concepts to perceptual data—and to prove the validity of scientific induction. . . . The philosophers were unable to refute the Witch Doctor's claim that their concepts were as arbitrary as his whims and that their scientific knowledge had no greater metaphysical validity than his revelations."

These are the reasons why I chose to introduce you to Objectivist epistemology by presenting my theory of concepts. I entitle this work an "Introduction," because the theory is presented outside of its full context. For instance, I do not include here a discussion of the validity of man's senses— since the arguments of those who attack the senses are merely variants of the fallacy of the "stolen concept."

For the purposes of this series, the validity of the senses must be taken for granted—and one must remember the axiom: *Existence exists.* (This, incidentally, is a way of translating into the form of a proposition, and thus into the form of an axiom, the primary fact which is existence.) Please bear in mind the full statement: "Existence exists— and the act of grasping that statement implies two corollary axioms: that something exists which one perceives and that one exists possessing consciousness, consciousness being the faculty of perceiving that which exists." (*Atlas Shrugged.*)

(For the reader's convenience, a summary of the text is provided at the conclusion of this work.)

—AYN RAND

New York, July 1966.

1. Cognition and Measurement

Consciousness, as a state of awareness, is not a passive state, but an active process that consists of two essentials: differentiation and integration.

Although, chronologically, man's consciousness develops in three stages: the stage of sensations, the perceptual, the conceptual—epistemologically, the base of all of man's knowledge is the *perceptual* stage.

Sensations, as such, are not retained in man's memory, nor is man able to experience a pure isolated sensation. As far as can be ascertained, an infant's sensory experience is an undifferentiated chaos. Discriminated awareness begins on the level of percepts.

A percept is a group of sensations automatically retained and integrated by the brain of a living organism. It is in the form of percepts that man grasps the evidence of his senses and apprehends reality. When we speak of "direct perception" or "direct awareness," we mean the perceptual level. Percepts, not sensations, are the given, the self-evident. The knowledge of sensations as components of percepts is not direct, it is acquired by man much later: it is a scientific, *conceptual* discovery.

The building-block of man's knowledge is the concept of an *"existent"*—of something that exists, be it a thing, an attribute or an action. Since it is a concept, man cannot grasp it *explicitly* until he has reached the conceptual stage. But it is implicit in every percept (to perceive a thing is to perceive that it exists) and man grasps it *implicitly* on the perceptual level—i.e., he grasps the constituents of the concept "existent," the data which are later to be integrated by that concept. It is this implicit knowledge that permits his consciousness to develop further.

(It may be supposed that the concept "existent" is implicit even on the level of sensations—if and to the extent that a consciousness is able to discriminate on that level. A sensation is a sensation of *something,* as distinguished from the *nothing* of the preceding and succeeding moments. A sensation does not tell man *what* exists, but only *that* it exists.)

The (implicit) concept *"existent"* undergoes three stages of development in man's mind. The first stage is a child's awareness of objects, of things—which represents the (implicit) concept *"entity."* The second and closely allied stage is the awareness of specific, particular things which he can recognize and distinguish from the rest of his perceptual field—which represents the (implicit) concept *"identity."*

The third stage consists of grasping relationships among these entities by grasping the similarities and differences of their identities. This requires the transformation of the (implicit) concept "entity" into the (implicit) concept "*unit.*"

When a child observes that two objects (which he will later learn to designate as "tables") resemble each other, but are different from four other objects ("chairs"), his mind is focusing on a particular attribute of the objects (their shape), then isolating them according to their differences, and integrating them as units into separate groups according to their similarities.

This is the key, the entrance to the conceptual level of man's consciousness. *The ability to regard entities as units is man's distinctive method of cognition*, which other living species are unable to follow.

A unit is an existent regarded as a separate member of a group of two or more similar members. (Two stones are two units; so are two square feet of ground, if regarded as distinct parts of a continuous stretch of ground.) Note that the concept "unit" involves an act of consciousness (a selective focus, a certain way of regarding things), but that it is *not* an arbitrary creation of consciousness: it is a method of identification or classification according to the attributes which a consciousness observes in reality. This method permits any number of classifications and cross-classifications: one may classify things according to their shape or color or weight or size or atomic structure; but the criterion of classification is not invented, it is perceived in reality. Thus the concept "unit" is a bridge between metaphysics and epistemology: units do not exist *qua* units, what exists are things, but *units are things viewed by a consciousness in certain existing relationships.*

With the grasp of the (implicit) concept "unit" man reaches the conceptual level of cognition, which consists of two interrelated fields: the *conceptual* and the *mathematical.* The process of concept-formation is, in large part, a mathematical process.

Mathematics is the science of *measurement.* Before proceeding to the subject of concept-formation, let us first consider the subject of measurement.

Measurement is the identification of a relationship—a quantitative relationship established by means of a standard that serves as a unit. Entities (and their actions) are measured by their attributes (length, weight, velocity, etc.) and the standard of measurement is a concretely specified unit representing the appropriate attribute. Thus, one measures length in inches, feet and miles—weight in pounds—velocity by means of a given distance traversed in a given time, etc.

It is important to note that while the choice of a given standard is optional, the mathematical rules of using it are not. It makes no difference whether one measures length in terms of feet or meters; the standard provides only the form of notation, not the substance nor the result of the process of measuring. The facts established by measurement will be the same, regardless of the particular standard used; the standard can neither alter nor affect them. The requirements of a standard of measurement are: that it represent the appropriate attribute, that it be easily perceivable by man and that, once chosen, it remain immutable and absolute whenever used. (Please remember this; we will have reason to recall it.)

Now what is the purpose of measurement? Observe that measurement consists of relating an easily perceivable unit to larger or smaller quantities, then to infinitely larger or infinitely smaller quantities, which are not directly perceivable to man. (The word "infinitely" is used here as a mathematical, not a metaphysical, term.) The purpose of measurement is to expand the range of man's consciousness, of his knowledge, beyond the perceptual level: beyond the direct power of his senses and the immediate concretes of any given moment. Man can perceive the length of one foot directly; he cannot perceive ten miles. By establishing the relationship of feet to miles, he can grasp and know any distance on earth; by establishing the relationship of miles to light-years, he can know the distances of galaxies.

The process of measurement is a process of integrating an unlimited scale of knowledge to man's limited perceptual experience—a process of making the universe knowable by bringing it within the range of man's consciousness, by establishing its relationship to man. It is not an accident that man's earliest attempts at measurement (the evidence of which survives to this day) consisted of relating things to *himself*—as, for instance, taking the length of his foot as a standard of length, or adopting the decimal system, which is supposed to have its origin in man's ten fingers as units of counting.

It is here that Protagoras' old dictum may be given a new meaning, the opposite of the one he intended: "Man is the measure of all things." Man *is* the measure, epistemologically—*not* metaphysically. In regard to human knowledge, man has to be the measure, since he has to bring all things into the realm of the humanly knowable. But, far from leading to subjectivism, the methods which he has to employ require the most rigorous mathematical precision, the most rigorous compliance with objective rules and facts—if the end product is to be *knowledge*.

This is true of mathematical principles and of the principles by which man forms his concepts. Man's mathematical and conceptual abilities develop simultaneously. A child learns to count when he is learning his first words. And in order to proceed beyond the stage of counting his ten fingers, it is the *conceptual* level of his consciousness that man has to expand.

2. Concept-Formation

A *concept* is a mental integration of two or more units which are isolated according to a specific characteristic(s) and united by a specific definition.

The units involved may be any aspect of reality: entities, attributes, actions, qualities, relationships, etc.; they may be perceptual concretes or other, earlier-formed concepts. The act of isolation involved is a process of *abstraction:* i.e., a selective mental focus that *takes out* or separates a certain aspect of reality from all others (e.g., isolates a certain attribute from the entities possessing it, or a certain action from the entities performing it, etc.). The uniting involved is not a mere sum, but an *integration*, i.e., a blending of the units into a *single*, new *mental* entity which is used thereafter as a single unit of thought (but which can be broken into its component units whenever required).

In order to be used as a single unit, the enormous sum integrated by a concept has to be given the form of a single, specific, *perceptual* concrete, which will differentiate it from all other concretes and from all other concepts. This is the function performed by language. Language is a code of visual-auditory symbols that serves the psycho-epistemological function of converting concepts into the mental equivalent of concretes. Language is the exclusive domain and tool of concepts. Every word we use (with the exception of proper names) is a symbol that denotes a concept, i.e., that stands for an unlimited number of concretes of a certain kind.

(Proper names are used in order to identify and include particular entities in a conceptual method of cognition. Observe that even proper names, in advanced civilizations, follow the definitional principles of *genus* and *differentia:* e.g., John Smith, with "Smith" serving as *genus* and "John" as *differentia*—or New York, U.S.A.)

Words transform concepts into (mental) entities; *definitions* provide them with *identity.* (Words without definitions are not language but inarticulate sounds.) We shall discuss definitions later and at length.

The above is a general description of the nature of concepts as products of a certain mental process. But *the* question of epistemology is: what precisely is the nature of that process? To what precisely do concepts refer in reality?

Let us now examine the process of forming the simplest concept, the concept of a single attribute (chronologically, this is not the first concept that a child would grasp; but it is the simplest one epistemologically)—for instance, the concept *"length."* If a child considers a match, a pencil and a stick, he observes that length is the attribute they have in common, but their specific lengths differ. The *difference is one of measurement.* In order to form the concept "length," the child's mind retains the attribute and omits its particular measurements. Or, more precisely, if the process were identified in words, it would consist of the following: "Length must exist in *some* quantity, but may exist in *any* quantity. I shall identify as 'length' that attribute of any existent possessing it which can be quantitatively related to a unit of length, without specifying the quantity."

The child does not think in such words (he has, as yet, no knowledge of words), but *that* is the nature of the process which his mind performs wordlessly. And that is the principle which his mind follows, when, having grasped the concept "length" by observing the three objects, he uses it to identify the attribute of length in a piece of string, a ribbon, a belt, a corridor or a street.

The same principle directs the process of forming concepts of entities—for instance, the concept "table." The child's mind isolates two or more tables from other objects, by focusing on their distinctive characteristic: their shape. He observes that their shapes vary, but have one characteristic in common: a flat, level surface and support(s). He forms the concept "table" by retaining that characteristic and omitting *all* particular measurements, not only the measurements of the shape, but of all the other characteristics of tables (many of which he is not aware of at the time).

An adult definition of "table" would be: "A man-made object consisting of a flat, level surface and support(s), intended to support other, smaller objects." Observe what is specified and what is omitted in this definition: the distinctive characteristic of the shape is specified and retained; the particular geometrical measurements of the shape (whether the surface is square, round, oblong or triangular, etc., the number and shape of supports, etc.) are omitted; the measurements of size or weight are omitted; the fact that it is a material object is specified, but the material of which it is made is omitted, thus omitting the measurements that differentiate one material from another; etc. Observe, however, that the utilitarian requirements of the table set certain limits on the omitted measurements, in the form of "no larger than and no smaller than" required by its purpose. This rules out a ten-foot tall or a two-inch tall table (though the latter may be sub-classified as a toy or a miniature table) and it rules out unsuitable materials, such as non-solids.

Bear firmly in mind that the term "measurements omitted" does not mean, in this context, that measurements are regarded as non-existent; it means that *measurements exist, but are not specified.* That measurements *must* exist is an essential part of the process. The principle is: the relevant measurements must exist in *some* quantity, but may exist in *any* quantity.

A child is not and does not have to be aware of all these complexities when he forms the concept "table." He forms it by differentiating tables from

all other objects *in the context of his knowledge.*
As his knowledge grows, the definitions of his
concepts grow in complexity. (We shall discuss
this when we discuss definitions.) But the principle and pattern of concept-formation remain the
same.

The first words a child learns are words denoting visual objects, and he retains his first concepts
visually. Observe that the visual form he gives
them is reduced to those *essentials* which distinguish the particular kind of entities from all others—for instance, the universal type of a child's
drawing of man in the form of an oval for the
torso, a circle for the head, four sticks for extrem-
ities, etc. Such drawings are a visual record of the
process of abstraction and concept-formation in a
mind's transition from the perceptual level to the
full vocabulary of the conceptual level.

There is evidence to suppose that written language originated in the form of drawings—as the
pictographic writing of the Oriental peoples seems
to indicate. With the growth of man's knowledge
and of his power of abstraction, a pictorial
representation of concepts could no longer be ade-
quate to his conceptual range, and was replaced
by a fully symbolic code.

*A concept is a mental integration of two or
more units possessing the same distinguishing
characteristic(s), with their particular measurements omitted.*

The element of *similarity* is crucially involved
in the formation of every concept; similarity, in
this context, is the relationship between two or

more existents which possess the same characteristic(s), but in different measure or degree.

Observe the multiple role of measurements in the process of concept-formation, in both of its two essential parts: differentiation and integration. Concepts cannot be formed at random. All concepts are formed by first differentiating two or more existents from other existents. All conceptual differentiations are made in terms of *commensurable characteristics* (i.e., characteristics possessing a common unit of measurement). No concept could be formed, for instance, by attempting to distinguish long objects from green objects. Incommensurable characteristics cannot be integrated into one unit.

Tables, for instance, are first differentiated from chairs, beds and other objects by means of the characteristic of *shape,* which is an attribute possessed by all the objects involved. Then, their particular kind of shape is set as the distinguishing characteristic of tables—i.e., a certain category of geometrical measurements of shape is specified. Then, within that category, the particular measurements of individual table-shapes are omitted.

Please note the fact that a given shape represents a certain category or set of geometrical measurements. Shape is an attribute; differences of shape—whether cubes, spheres, cones or any complex combinations—are a matter of differing measurements; any shape can be reduced to or expressed by a set of figures in terms of *linear measurement.* When, in the process of concept-formation, man observes that shape is a commensurable characteristic of certain objects, he does not have to measure all the shapes involved *nor even to know how to measure them;* he merely has to observe the element of *similarity.*

Similarity is grasped *perceptually;* in observing it, man is not and does not have to be aware of the fact that it involves a matter of measurement. It is the task of philosophy and of science to identify that fact.

As to the actual process of measuring shapes, a vast part of higher mathematics, from geometry on up, is devoted to the task of discovering methods by which various shapes can be measured—complex methods which consist of reducing the problem to the terms of a simple, primitive method, the only one available to man in this field: linear measurement. (Integral calculus, used to measure the area of circles, is just one example.)

In this respect, concept-formation and applied mathematics have a similar task, just as philosophical epistemology and theoretical mathematics have a similar goal: the goal and task of bringing the universe within the range of man's knowledge—by identifying relationships to perceptual data.

Another example of implicit measurement can be seen in the process of forming concepts of colors. Man forms such concepts by observing that the various shades of blue are similar, as against the shades of red, and thus differentiating the range of blue from the range of red, of yellow, etc.

Centuries passed before science discovered the unit by which colors could actually be measured: the wavelengths of light—a discovery that supported, in terms of mathematical proof, the differentiations that men were and are making in terms of visual similarities. (Any questions about "borderline cases" will be answered later.)

A commensurable characteristic (such as shape in the case of tables, or hue in the case of colors) is an essential element in the process of concept-formation. I shall designate it as the "Conceptual Common Denominator" and define it as "The characteristic(s) reducible to a unit of measurement, by means of which man differentiates two or more existents from other existents possessing it."

The distinguishing characteristic(s) of a concept represents a specified category of measurements within the "Conceptual Common Denominator" involved.

New concepts can be formed by integrating earlier-formed concepts into wider categories, or by subdividing them into narrower categories (a process which we shall discuss later). But all concepts are ultimately reducible to their base in perceptual entities, which are the base (the given) of man's cognitive development.

The first concepts man forms are concepts of entities—since entities are the only primary existents. (Attributes cannot exist by themselves, they are merely the characteristics of entities; motions are motions of entities; relationships are relationships among entities.)

In the process of forming concepts of entities, a child's mind has to focus on a distinguishing characteristic—i.e., on an attribute—in order to isolate one group of entities from all others. He is, therefore, aware of attributes while forming his first concepts, but he is aware of them *perceptually, not* conceptually. It is only after he has grasped a number of concepts of entities that he can advance to the stage of abstracting attributes from entities and forming separate concepts of attributes. The same is true of concepts of motion: a child is aware of motion *perceptually,* but cannot conceptualize "motion" until he has formed some concepts of that which moves, i.e., of entities.

(As far as can be ascertained, the perceptual level of a child's awareness is similar to the awareness of the higher animals: the higher animals are able to perceive entities, motions, attributes, and certain numbers of entities. But what an animal cannot perform is the process of abstraction—of mentally separating attributes, motions or numbers from entities. It has been said that an animal can perceive two oranges or two potatoes, but cannot grasp the concept "two.")

Concepts of *materials* are formed by observing the differences in the constituent materials of entities. (Materials exist only in the form of specific entities, such as a nugget of gold, a plank of wood, a drop or an ocean of water.) The concept of "gold," for instance, is formed by isolating gold objects from all others, then abstracting and retaining the material, the gold, and omitting the measurements of the objects (or of the alloys) in which gold may exist. Thus, the material is the same in all the concrete instances subsumed under the concept, and differs only in quantity.

Concepts of *motion* are formed by specifying the distinctive nature of the motion and of the entities performing it, and/or of the medium in which it is performed—and omitting the particular measurements of any given instance of such motion and of the entities involved. For instance, the concept "walking" denotes a certain kind of motion performed by living entities possessing legs, and does not apply to the motion of a snake or of an automobile. The concept "swimming" denotes the motion of any living entity propelling itself through water, and does not apply to the motion of a boat. The concept "flying" denotes the motion of any entity propelling itself through the air, whether a bird or an airplane.

Adverbs are concepts of the characteristics of motion (or action); they are formed by specifying a characteristic and omitting the measurements of the motion and of the entities involved—e.g., "rapidly," which may be applied to "walking" or "swimming" or "speaking," etc., with the measurement of what is "rapid" left open and depending, in any given case, on the type of motion involved.

Prepositions are concepts of relationships, predominantly of spatial or temporal relationships, among existents; they are formed by specifying the relationship and omitting the measurements of the existents and of the space or time involved—e.g., "on," "in," "above," "after," etc.

Adjectives are concepts of attributes or of characteristics. *Pronouns* belong to the category of concepts of entities. *Conjunctions* are concepts of relationships among thoughts, and belong to the category of concepts of consciousness.

As to concepts of consciousness, we shall discuss them later and at length. (To anticipate questions such as: "Can you measure love?"—I shall permit myself the very philosophical answer: "And how!")

Now we can answer the question: To what precisely do we refer when we designate three persons as "men"? We refer to the fact that they are living beings who possess the *same* characteristic distinguishing them from all other living species: a rational faculty—though the specific measurements of their distinguishing characteristic *qua* men, as well as of all their other characteristics *qua* living beings, are different. (As living beings of a certain kind, they possess innumerable characteristics in common: the same shape, the same range of size, the same facial features, the same vital organs, the same fingerprints, etc., and all these characteristics differ only in their measurements.)

Two links between the conceptual and the mathematical fields are worth noting at this point, apart from the obvious fact that the concept "unit" is the base and start of both.

1. A concept is not formed by observing every concrete subsumed under it, and does not specify the number of such concretes. A concept is like an arithmetical sequence of *specifically defined units,* going off in both directions, open at both ends and including *all* units of that particular kind. For in-

stance, the concept "man" includes all men who live at present, who have ever lived or will ever live. An arithmetical sequence extends into infinity, without implying that infinity actually exists; such extension means only that whatever number of units does exist, it is to be included in the same sequence. The same principle applies to concepts: the concept "man" does not (and need not) specify what number of men will ultimately have existed— it specifies only the characteristics of man, and means that any number of entities possessing these characteristics is to be identified as "men."

2. The basic principle of concept-formation (which states that the omitted measurements must exist in *some* quantity, but may exist in *any* quantity) is the equivalent of the basic principle of algebra, which states that algebraic symbols must be given *some* numerical value, but may be given *any* value. In this sense and respect, perceptual awareness is the arithmetic, but *conceptual awareness is the algebra of cognition.*

The relationship of concepts to their constituent particulars is the same as the relationship of algebraic symbols to numbers. In the equation $2a = a + a$, any number may be substituted for the symbol "a" without affecting the truth of the equation. For instance: $2 \times 5 = 5 + 5$, or: $2 \times 5,000,000 = 5,000,000 + 5,000,000$. In the same manner, by the same psycho-epistemological method, a concept is used as an algebraic symbol that stands for *any* of the arithmetical sequence of units it subsumes.

Let those who attempt to invalidate concepts by declaring that they cannot find "manness" in men, try to invalidate algebra by declaring that they cannot find "*a*-ness" in 5 or in 5,000,000.

3. Abstraction from Abstractions

Starting from the base of conceptual development—from the concepts that identify perceptual concretes—the process of cognition moves in two interacting directions: toward more extensive and more intensive knowledge, toward wider integrations and more precise differentiations. Following the process and *in accordance with cognitive evidence,* earlier-formed concepts are integrated into wider ones or subdivided into narrower ones.

The role of language (which we shall discuss at length when we discuss definitions) must be mentioned briefly at this point. The process of forming a concept is not complete until its constituent units have been integrated into a single mental unit by means of a specific word. The first concepts a child forms are concepts of perceptual entities; the first words he learns are words designating them. Even though a child does not have to perform the feat of genius performed by some mind or minds in the prehistorical infancy of the human race: the invention of language—every child has to perform independently the feat of grasping the nature of language, the process of symbolizing concepts by means of words.

Even though a child does not (and need not) originate and form every concept on his own, by observing every aspect of reality confronting him, he has to perform the process of differentiating and integrating perceptual concretes, in order to grasp the meaning of words. If a child's brain is physically damaged and unable to perform that process, he does not learn to speak.

Learning to speak does not consist of memorizing sounds—*that* is the process by which a parrot learns to "speak." Learning consists of grasping meanings, i.e., of grasping the *referents* of words, the kinds of existents that words denote in reality. In this respect, the learning of words is an invaluable accelerator of a child's cognitive development, but it is not a substitute for the process of concept-formation; nothing is.

After the first stage of learning certain fundamentals, there is no particular order in which a child learns new concepts; there is, for a while, a broad area of the optional, where he may learn simple, primary concepts and complex, derivative ones almost concurrently, depending on his own mental initiative and on the random influences of his environment. The particular order in which he learns new words is of no significance, at this stage, *provided he understands their meanings.* His full, independent conceptual development does not begin until he has acquired a sufficient vocabulary to be able to form sentences—i.e., *to be able to think* (at which time he can gradually bring order to his haphazard conceptual equipment). Up to that time, he is able to retain the referents of his concepts by perceptual, predominantly visual means; as his conceptual chain moves farther and farther away from perceptual concretes, the issue of verbal definitions becomes crucial. It is at this point that all hell breaks loose.

Apart from the fact that the educational methods of most of his elders are such that, instead of helping him, they tend to cripple his further development, a child's own choice and motivation are crucial at this point. There are many different ways in which children proceed to learn new words thereafter. Some (a very small minority) proceed straight on, by the same method as before, i.e., by treating words as concepts, by requiring a clear, first-hand understanding *(within the context of their knowledge)* of the exact meaning of every word they learn, never allowing a break in the chain linking their concepts to the facts of reality. Some proceed by the road of approximations, where the fog deepens with every step, where the use of words is guided by the feeling: "I kinda know what I mean." Some switch from cognition to imitation, substituting memorizing for understanding, and adopt something as close to a parrot's psycho-epistemology as a human brain can come—learning, not concepts nor words, but strings of sounds whose referents are not the facts of reality, but the facial expressions and emotional vibrations of their elders. And some (the overwhelming majority) adopt a precarious mixture of different degrees of all three methods.

But the question of how particular men happen to *learn* concepts and the question of what concepts *are,* are two different issues. In considering the nature of concepts and the process of abstracting from abstractions, we must assume a mind capable of performing (or of retracing and checking) that process. And we must remember that no matter how many men mouth a concept as a meaningless sound, *some* man had to originate it at some time.

The first stages of integrating concepts into wider concepts are fairly simple, because they still refer to perceptual concretes. For instance, man observes that the objects which he has identified by the concepts "table," "chair," "bed," "cabinet," etc. have certain similarities, but are different from the objects he has identified as "door," "window," "picture," "drapes"—and he integrates the former into the wider concept "furniture." In this process, concepts serve as units and are treated *epistemologically* as if each were a single (mental) concrete—always remembering that *metaphysically* (i.e., in reality) each unit stands for an unlimited number of actual concretes of a certain kind.

The distinguishing characteristics of these units are specified categories of measurements of shape, such as "a flat, level surface and support(s)" in the case of tables. In relation to the new concept, these distinguishing characteristics are now regarded in the same manner as the measurements of individual table-shapes were regarded in forming the concept "table": they are omitted, on the principle that a piece of furniture must have *some* shape, but may have *any* of the shapes characterizing the various units subsumed under the new concept.

The *distinguishing* characteristic of the new concept is determined by the nature of the objects from which its constituent units are being differentiated, i.e., by their "Conceptual Common Denominator," which, in this case, is: large objects inside a human habitation. The adult definition of "furniture" would be: "Movable man-made objects intended to be used in a human habitation, which can support the weight of the human body or support and/or store other, smaller objects." This differentiates "furniture" from architectural features, such as doors or windows, from ornamental objects, such as pictures or drapes, and from a variety of smaller objects that may be used inside a habitation, such as ashtrays, bric-a-brac, dishes, etc.

The distinguishing characteristics of "furniture" are a specified range of functions in a specified place (both are measurable characteristics): "furniture" must be no larger than can be placed inside a human habitation, no smaller than can perform the specified functions, etc.

Observe that the concept "furniture" is an abstraction one step further removed from perceptual reality than any of its constituent concepts. "Table" is an abstraction, since it designates *any* table, but its meaning can be conveyed simply by pointing to one or two perceptual objects. There is no such perceptual object as "furniture"; there are only tables, chairs, beds, etc. The meaning of "furniture" cannot be grasped unless one has first grasped the meaning of its constituent concepts;

these are its link to reality. (On the lower levels of an unlimited conceptual chain, this is an illustration of the hierarchical structure of concepts.)

Observe also that the concept "furniture" involves a relationship to another concept, which is not one of its constituent units, but which has to be grasped before one can grasp the meaning of "furniture": the concept "habitation." This kind of interrelationship among concepts grows progressively more complex as the level of concept-formation grows farther away from perceptual concretes.

Now let us examine the process of subdividing the concept "table." By observing the differences in the size and function of various tables, man subdivides the concept into: "dining table," "coffee table," "end table," "desk," etc. In the first three instances, the distinguishing characteristic of "table," its shape, is retained, and the differentiations are purely a matter of measurement: the range of the shape's measurements is reduced in accordance with the narrower utilitarian function. (Coffee tables are lower and smaller than dining tables; end tables are higher than coffee tables, but lower than dining tables, etc.) In the case of "desk," however, the distinguishing characteristic of "table" is retained, but combined with a new element: a "desk" is a table with drawers for storing stationery supplies. The first three instances are not actually new concepts, but qualified instances of the concept "table." "Desk," however, involves a significant difference in its distinguishing characteristic, it involves an additional category of measurements, and is given a new linguistic symbol. (As far as the process of concept-formation is concerned, it would make no difference if "desk" were designated as "office table," or if a new word were coined for each of the other sub-categories of "table." There is, however, an epistemological reason for the present designations, which we shall discuss when we discuss definitions.)

When concepts are integrated into a wider one, the new concept includes *all* the characteristics of its constituent units; but their distinguishing characteristics are regarded as omitted measurements, and one of their common characteristics determines the distinguishing characteristic of the new concept: the one representing their "Conceptual Common Denominator" with the existents from which they are being differentiated.

When a concept is subdivided into narrower ones, its distinguishing characteristic is taken as their "Conceptual Common Denominator"—and is given a narrower range of specified measurements or is combined with an additional characteristic(s), to form the individual distinguishing characteristics of the new concepts.

Let us observe these two principles on another example: the ramifications of the concept "man."

Man's particular type of consciousness is the distinguishing characteristic by which a child (at a certain level of development) differentiates him from all other entities. By observing the similarities among "cat," "dog," "horse," "bird," and by differentiating them from other entities, he integrates them into the wider concept "animal"—and, later, includes "man" in this wider concept. The definition of "animal" (in general terms) would be: "A living entity possessing the faculties of consciousness and locomotion."

Man's distinguishing characteristic, his rational faculty, is omitted from the definition of "animal"—on the principle that an animal must possess *some* type of consciousness, but may possess *any* of the types characterizing the various units subsumed under the new concept. (The standard of measurement that differentiates one type of consciousness from another is its *range*.)

The distinguishing characteristics of the new concept are characteristics possessed by all its constituent units: the attribute "living" and the faculties "consciousness and locomotion."

With further knowledge, by observing the similarities among animals, plants and certain sub-microscopic entities (and their differences from inanimate objects), man integrates them into the concept "organism." The definition of "organism" (in general terms) would be: "An entity possessing the capacities of internally generated action, of growth through metabolism, and of reproduction."

These distinguishing characteristics of the new concept are possessed by all its constituent units. The distinguishing characteristics of "animal" are omitted from the definition—on the principle that the "internally generated actions" must exist in *some* form (including "consciousness and locomotion"), but may exist in *any* of the forms characterizing the various units subsumed under the new concept.

With the growth of man's knowledge, a very broad concept, such as "animal," is subdivided into new concepts, such as: "mammal," "amphibian," "fish," "bird," etc. Each of these is then subdivided further and further into narrower sub-categories. The principle of concept-formation remains the same: the distinguishing characteristics of the concept "animal" (the faculties of "consciousness and locomotion") are the "Conceptual Common Denominator" of these subdivisions, and are retained but qualified by the addition of other (anatomical and physiological) characteristics to form the distinguishing characteristics of the new concepts.

(The chronological order in which man forms or learns these concepts is optional. A child, for instance, may first integrate the appropriate concretes into the concepts "animal," "bird," "fish," then later integrate them into a wider concept by expanding his concept of "animal." The principles involved and the ultimate choice of distinguishing characteristics will be the same, granting he reaches the same level of knowledge.)

Turning now to the process of conceptual subdivision, the concept "man" can be subdivided into innumerable sub-categories, according to various aspects or attributes. For instance, such concepts as "child," "adolescent," "youth," "adult" are formed according to measurements of time, i.e., according to the number of years lived. These concepts retain the distinguishing characteristic of "rational animal" but narrowed by a specified range of years.

The concept "man" can be subdivided according to special characteristics, such as racial (anatomical) descent: "Caucasian," "Negro," "Mongolian," etc.—or national (politico-geographical) origin: "American," "Englishman," "Frenchman," etc.—or professional activity: "Engineer," "Doctor," "Artist," etc. (which involve concepts of consciousness)—or even according to such characteristics as the color of hair: "Blonde," "Brunette," "Redhead." In all such cases, the distinguishing characteristic of "rational animal" is retained but narrowed by specified characteristics which represent specified categories of measurements.

The concept "man" can be subdivided according to special relationships—for instance, according to a biological relationship ("Father," "Son," "Brother"), or a legal relationship ("Husband, "Wife"), or an economic relationship ("Employer," "Employee"), etc. In all such cases, the characteristic of "rational animal" is retained but combined with a specified relationship.

Some concepts of relationships (such as "legal" or "economic") involve concepts of consciousness. The most complex abstractions (both in regard to wider integrations and narrower subdivisions) are those which involve a combination of concepts of action with concepts of consciousness. (We shall discuss these in the next chapter.)

Two aspects of the cognitive content of abstractions are worth noting at this point.

1. The formation (or the learning) of wider

concepts requires more knowledge (i.e., a wider range of conceptualized evidence) than was required by any one of the constituent concepts which they subsume. For instance, the concept "animal" requires more knowledge than the concept "man"—since it requires knowledge of man and of some of the other species. It requires a sufficient knowledge of man's characteristics and of the characteristics of other animals to differentiate man from other animals, and to differentiate animals from plants or from inanimate objects.

A widespread error, in this context, holds that the wider the concept, the less its cognitive content —on the ground that its distinguishing characteristic is more generalized than the distinguishing characteristics of its constituent concepts. The error lies in assuming that a concept consists of nothing but its distinguishing characteristic. But the fact is that in the process of abstracting from abstractions, one cannot know *what* is a distinguishing characteristic unless one has observed other characteristics of the units involved and of the existents from which they are differentiated.

Just as the concept "man" does not consist merely of "rational faculty" (if it did, the two would be equivalent and interchangeable, which they are not), but includes *all* the characteristics of "man," with "rational faculty" serving as the distinguishing characteristic—so, in the case of wider concepts, the concept "animal" does not consist merely of "consciousness and locomotion," but subsumes *all* the characteristics of all the animal species, with "consciousness and locomotion" serving as the distinguishing characteristic. (We shall discuss this further when we discuss definitions.)

An error of that kind is possible only on the basis of assuming that man learns concepts by memorizing their definitions, i.e., on the basis of studying the epistemology of a parrot. But that is not what we are here studying. To grasp a concept is to grasp and, in part, to retrace the process by which it was formed. To retrace that process is to grasp at least *some* of the units which it subsumes (and thus to link one's understanding of the concept to the facts of reality).

Just as wider integrations of concepts require a more *extensive* knowledge, so narrower subdivisions of concepts require a more *intensive* knowledge. For instance, the concept "father" requires more knowledge than the concept "man"—since it requires knowledge of man, of the act of reproduction, and of the consequent relationship.

2. The formation of a concept provides man with the means of identifying, not only the concretes he has observed, but all the concretes *of that kind* which he may encounter in the future. Thus, when he has formed or grasped the concept "man," he does not have to regard every man he meets thereafter as a new phenomenon to be studied from scratch: he identifies him as "man" and applies to him the knowledge he has acquired about man (which leaves him free to study the particular, individual characteristics of the newcomer, i.e., the individual measurements within the categories established by the concept "man").

This process of conceptual identification (of subsuming a new concrete under an appropriate concept) is learned as one learns to speak, and it becomes automatic in the case of existents given in perceptual awareness, such as "man," "table," "blue," "length," etc. But it grows progressively more difficult as man's concepts move farther away from direct perceptual evidence, and involve complex combinations and cross-classifications of many earlier concepts. (Observe the difficulties of identifying a given political system, or of diagnosing a rare disease.) In such cases, the knowledge of whether a concrete is or is not to be subsumed under a certain concept does not come automatically, but requires a new cognitive effort.

Thus the process of forming and applying concepts contains the essential pattern of two fundamental methods of cognition: *induction* and *deduction*.

The process of observing the facts of reality and of integrating them into concepts is, in essence, a process of induction. The process of subsuming new instances under a known concept is, in essence, a process of deduction.

4. Concepts of Consciousness

Consciousness is the faculty of awareness—the faculty of perceiving that which exists.

Awareness is not a passive state, but an active process. On the lower levels of awareness, a complex neurological process is required to enable man to experience a sensation and to integrate sensations into percepts; that process is automatic and non-volitional: man is aware of its results, but not of the process itself. On the higher, conceptual level, the process is psychological, conscious and volitional. In either case, awareness is achieved and maintained by continuous *action*.

Directly or indirectly, every phenomenon of consciousness is derived from one's awareness of the external world. Some object, i.e., some *content*, is involved in every state of awareness. Extrospection is a process of cognition directed outward—a process of apprehending some existent(s) of the external world. Introspection is a process of cognition directed inward—a process of apprehending one's own psychological actions in regard to some existent(s) of the external world, such actions as thinking, feeling, reminiscing, etc. It is only in relation to the external world that the various actions of a consciousness can be experienced, grasped, defined or communicated. Awareness is awareness of something. A content-less state of consciousness is a contradiction in terms.

Two fundamental attributes are involved in every state, aspect or function of man's consciousness: content and action—the content of awareness, and the action of consciousness in regard to that content.

These two attributes are the fundamental Conceptual Common Denominator of all concepts pertaining to consciousness.

On the perceptual level of awareness, a child merely experiences and performs various psychological processes; his full conceptual development requires that he learn to conceptualize them (after he has reached a certain stage in his extrospective conceptual development).

To form concepts of consciousness, one must isolate the action from the content of a given state of consciousness, by a process of abstraction. Just as, extrospectively, man can abstract attributes from entities—so, introspectively, he can abstract the actions of his consciousness from its contents, and observe the *differences* among these various actions.

For instance (on the adult level), when a man sees a woman walking down the street, the action of his consciousness is *perception;* when he notes that she is beautiful, the action of his consciousness is *evaluation;* when he experiences an inner state of pleasure and approval, of admiration, the action of his consciousness is *emotion;* when he stops to watch her and draws conclusions, from the evidence, about her character, age, social position, etc., the action of his consciousness is *thought;* when, later, he recalls the incident, the action of his consciousness is *reminiscence;* when he projects that her appearance would be improved if her hair were blond rather than brown, and her dress were blue rather than red, the action of his consciousness is *imagination.*

He can also observe the *similarities* among the actions of his consciousness on various occasions, by observing the fact that these same actions—in different sequences, combinations and degrees—are, have been or can be applicable to other objects: to a man, a dog, an automobile, or the entire street; to the reading of a book, the learning of a new skill, the choice of a job, or to any object within the scope of his awareness.

Such is the pattern of the process by which (in slower, gradual steps) man learns to form concepts of consciousness.

In the realm of introspection, the concretes, the *units* which are integrated into a single concept, are the specific instances of a given psychological process. The measurable attributes of a psychological process are its object or *content* and its *intensity.*

The content is some aspect of the external world (or is derived from some aspect of the external world) and is measurable by the various methods of measurement applicable to the external world. The intensity of a psychological process is the automatically summed up result of many factors: of its scope, its clarity, its cognitive and motivational context, the degree of mental energy or effort required, etc.

There is no exact method of measuring the intensity of all psychological processes, but—as in the case of forming concepts of colors—conceptualization does not require the knowledge of exact measurements. Degrees of intensity can be and are measured approximately, on a comparative scale. For instance, the intensity of the emotion of joy in response to certain facts varies according to the importance of these facts in one's *hierarchy* of values; it varies in such cases as buying a new suit, or getting a raise in pay, or marrying the person one loves. The intensity of a process of thought and of the intellectual effort required varies according to the *scope* of its content; it varies when one grasps the concept "table" or the concept "justice," when one grasps that $2 + 2 = 4$ or that $e = mc^2$.

The formation of introspective concepts follows the same principles as the formation of extrospective concepts. A concept pertaining to consciousness is a mental integration of two or more instances of a psychological process possessing the same distinguishing characteristics, with the particular contents and the measurements of the action's intensity omitted—on the principle that these omitted measurements must exist in *some* quantity, but may exist in *any* quantity (i.e., a given psychological process must possess *some* content and *some* degree of intensity, but may possess *any* content or degree of the appropriate category).

For instance, the concept "thought" is formed by retaining the distinguishing characteristics of the psychological action (a purposefully directed process of cognition) and by omitting the particular contents as well as the degree of the intellectual effort's intensity. The concept "emotion" is formed by retaining the distinguishing characteristics of the psychological action (an automatic response proceeding from an evaluation of an existent) and by omitting the particular contents (the existents) as well as the degree of emotional intensity.

Now observe that I have mentioned the terms *scope* and *hierarchy* in connection with the intensity of psychological processes. These are terms that belong to the category of measurements—and they indicate more precise methods of measuring some psychological phenomena.

In regard to the concepts pertaining to cognition ("thought," "observation," "reasoning," "learning," etc.), the scope of the content provides a method of measurement. The scope is gauged by two interrelated aspects: by the scope of the factual material involved in a given cognitive process, and by *the length of the conceptual chain* required to deal with that material. Since concepts have a hierarchical structure, i.e., since the higher, more complex abstractions are derived from the simpler, basic ones (starting with the concepts of perceptually given concretes), the distance from the perceptual level of the concepts used in a given cognitive process indicates the scope of that process. (The level of abstraction with which a man is able to deal indicates how much he had to know in order to reach that level. I am not speaking here of men who mouth memorized floating abstractions, but only of those who actually grasp all the steps involved.)

In regard to the concepts pertaining to evaluation ("value," "emotion," "feeling," "desire," etc.), the hierarchy involved is of a different kind and requires an entirely different type of measurement. It is a type applicable only to the psychological process of evaluation, and may be designated as *"teleological measurement."*

Measurement is the identification of a relationship—a quantitative relationship established by means of a standard that serves as a unit. Teleological measurement deals, not with cardinal, but with *ordinal* numbers—and the standard serves to establish a graded relationship of means to end.

For instance, a moral code is a system of teleological measurement which grades the choices and actions open to man, according to the degree to which they achieve or frustrate the code's standard of value. The standard is the end, to which man's actions are the means.

A moral code is a set of abstract principles; to practice it, an individual must translate it into the appropriate concretes—he must choose the particular goals and values which he is to pursue. This requires that he define his particular hierarchy of values, in the order of their importance, and that he act accordingly. Thus all his actions have to be guided by a process of teleological measurement. (The degree of uncertainty and contradictions in a man's hierarchy of values is the degree to which he will be unable to perform such measurements and will fail in his attempts at value calculations or at purposeful action.)

Teleological measurement has to be performed in and against an enormous context: it consists of establishing the relationship of a given choice to all the other possible choices and to one's hierarchy of values.

The simplest example of this process, which all men practice (with various degrees of precision and success), may be seen in the realm of material values—in the (implicit) principles that guide a man's spending of money. On any level of income, a man's money is a limited quantity; in spending it, he weighs the value of his purchase against the value of every other purchase open to him for the same amount of money, he weighs it against the hierarchy of all his other goals, desires and needs, then makes the purchase or not accordingly.

The same kind of measurement guides man's actions in the wider realm of moral or spiritual values. (By "spiritual" I mean "pertaining to consciousness." I say "wider" because it is man's hierarchy of values in this realm that determines his hierarchy of values in the material or economic realm.) But the currency or medium of exchange is different. In the spiritual realm, the currency—which exists in limited quantity and must be teleologically measured in the pursuit of any value—is *time*, i.e., *one's life.*

Since a value is that which one acts to gain and/or keep, and the amount of possible action is limited by the duration of one's lifespan, it is a part of one's life that one invests in everything one values. The years, months, days or hours of thought, of interest, of action devoted to a value are the currency with which one pays for the enjoyment one receives from it.

Now let us answer the question: "Can you measure love?"

The concept "love" is formed by isolating two or more instances of the appropriate psychological process, then retaining its distinguishing characteristics (an emotion proceeding from the evaluation of an existent as a positive value and as a source of pleasure) and omitting the object and the measurements of the process's intensity.

The object may be a thing, **an** event, an activity, a condition or a person. The intensity varies according to one's evaluation of the object, as, for instance, in such cases as one's love for ice cream, or for parties, or for reading, or for freedom, or for the person one marries. The concept "love" subsumes a vast range of values and, consequently, of intensity: it extends from the lower levels (designated by the sub-category "liking") to the higher level (designated by the sub-category "affection," which is applicable only in regard to persons) to the highest level, which includes romantic love.

If one wants to measure the intensity of a par-

ticular instance of love, one does so by reference
to the hierarchy of values of the person experienc-
ing it. A man may love a woman, yet may rate the
neurotic satisfactions of sexual promiscuity higher
than her value to him. Another man may love a
woman, but may give her up, rating his fear of
the disapproval of others (of his family, his friends
or any random strangers) higher than her value.
Still another man may risk his life to save the
woman he loves, because all his other values
would lose meaning without her. The emotions in
these examples are not emotions of the same intensity or dimension. Do not let a James Taggart
type of mystic tell you that love is immeasurable.

Certain categories of concepts of consciousness
require special consideration. These are concepts
pertaining to the *products* of psychological
processes, such as "knowledge," "science," "idea,"
etc.

These concepts are formed by retaining their
distinguishing characteristics and omitting their
content. For instance, the concept "knowledge" is
formed by retaining its distinguishing characteristics (a mental grasp of a fact(s) of reality, reached
either by perceptual observation or by a process of
reason based on perceptual observation) and omitting the particular fact(s) involved.

The intensity of the psychological processes
which led to the products is irrelevant here, but
the *nature* of these processes is included in the
distinguishing characteristics of the concepts, and
serves to differentiate the various concepts of this
kind.

It is important to note that these concepts are not the equivalent of their existential content—and that they belong to the category of epistemological concepts, with their metaphysical component regarded as their content. For instance, the concept "the science of physics" is not the same thing as the physical phenomena which are the content of the science. The phenomena exist independent of man's knowledge; the science is an organized body of knowledge about these phenomena, acquired by and communicable to a human consciousness. The phenomena would continue to exist, even if no human consciousness remained in existence; the science would not.

A special sub-category of concepts pertaining to the products of consciousness, is reserved for concepts of *method*. Concepts of method designate systematic courses of action devised by men for the purpose of achieving certain goals. The course of action may be purely psychological (such as a method of using one's consciousness) or it may involve a combination of psychological and physical actions (such as a method of drilling for oil), according to the goal to be achieved.

Concepts of method are formed by retaining the distinguishing characteristics of the purposive course of action and of its goal, while omitting the particular measurements of both.

For instance, *the* fundamental concept of method, the one on which all the others depend, is *logic*. The distinguishing characteristic of logic (the art of non-contradictory identification) indicates the nature of the actions (actions of consciousness required to achieve a correct identification) and their goal (knowledge)—while omitting the length, complexity or specific steps of the process of logical inference, as well as the nature of the particular cognitive problem involved in any given instance of using logic.

Concepts of method represent a large part of man's conceptual equipment. Epistemology is a science devoted to the discovery of the proper methods of acquiring and validating knowledge. Ethics is a science devoted to the discovery of the proper methods of living one's life. Medicine is a science devoted to the discovery of the proper methods of curing disease. All the applied sciences (i.e., technology) are sciences devoted to the discovery of methods.

The concepts of method are the link to the vast and complex category of concepts that represent integrations of existential concepts with concepts of consciousness, a category that includes most of the concepts pertaining to man's actions. Concepts of this category have no direct referents on the perceptual level of awareness (though they include perceptual components) and can neither be formed nor grasped without a long antecedent chain of concepts.

For instance, the concept "marriage" denotes a certain moral-legal relationship between a man and a woman, which entails a certain pattern of behavior, based on a mutual agreement and sanctioned by law. The concept "marriage" cannot be formed or grasped merely by observing the behavior of a couple: it requires the integration of their actions with a number of concepts of consciousness, such as "contractual agreement," "morality" and "law."

The concept "property" denotes the relationship of a man to an object (or an idea): his right to use it and to dispose of it—and involves a long chain of moral-legal concepts, including the procedure by which the object was acquired. The mere observation of a man in the act of using an object will not convey the concept "property."

Composite concepts of this kind are formed by isolating the appropriate existents, relationships, and actions, then retaining their distinguishing characteristics and omitting the type of measurements appropriate to the various categories of concepts involved.

Now a word about grammar. Grammar is a science dealing with the formulation of the proper methods of verbal expression and communication, i.e., the methods of organizing words (concepts) into sentences. Grammar pertains to the actions of consciousness, and involves a number of special concepts—such as conjunctions, which are concepts denoting relationships among thoughts ("and," "but," "or," etc.). These concepts are formed by retaining the distinguishing characteristics of the relationship and omitting the particular thoughts involved. The purpose of conjunctions is verbal economy: they serve to integrate and/or condense the content of certain thoughts.

For instance, the word "and" serves to integrate a number of facts into one thought. If one says: "Smith, Jones and Brown are walking," the "and" indicates that the observation "are walking" applies to the three individuals named. Is there an object in reality corresponding to the word "and"? No. Is there a fact in reality corresponding to the word "and"? Yes. The fact is that three men are walking—and that the word "and" integrates into one thought a fact which otherwise would have to be expressed by: "Smith is walking. Jones is walking. Brown is walking."

The word "but" serves to indicate an exception to or a contradiction of the possible implications of a given thought. If one says: "She is beautiful, but dumb," the "but" serves to condense the following thoughts: "This girl is beautiful. Beauty is a positive attribute, a value. Before you conclude that this girl is valuable, you must consider also her negative attribute: she is dumb." If one says: "I work every day, but not on Sunday," the "but" indicates an exception and condenses the following: "I work on Monday. I work on Tuesday. (And so on, four more times.) My activity on Sunday is different: I do not work on Sunday."

(These examples are for the benefit of those victims of modern philosophy who are taught by Linguistic Analysis that there is no way to derive conjunctions from experience, i.e., from the facts of reality.)

A certain aspect of the epistemological state of today's culture is worth noting at this point.

Observe that the attacks on the conceptual level of man's consciousness, i.e., on reason, come from the same ideological quarters as the attacks on *measurement*. When discussing man's consciousness, particularly his emotions, some persons use the word "measurement" as a pejorative term—as if an attempt to apply it to the phenomena of consciousness were a gross, insulting, "materialistic" impropriety. The question "Can you measure love?" is an example and a symptom of that attitude.

As in many other issues, the two allegedly opposite camps are merely two variants growing out of the same basic premises. The old-fashioned mystics proclaim that you cannot measure love in pounds, inches or dollars. They are aided and abetted by the neo-mystics who—punch-drunk with undigested concepts of measurement, proclaiming measurement to be the sole tool of science—proceed to measure knee-jerks, statistical questionnaires, and the learning time of rats, as indices to the human psyche.

Both camps fail to observe that *measurement requires an appropriate standard,* and that in the physical sciences—which one camp passionately hates, and the other passionately envies—one does not measure length in pounds, or weight in inches.

Measurement is the identification of a relationship in numerical terms—and the complexity of the science of measurement indicates the complexity of the relationships which exist in the universe and which man has barely begun to investigate. They exist, even if the appropriate standards and methods of measurement are not always as easily apparent nor the degree of achievable precision as great as in the case of measuring the basic, perceptually given attributes of matter. If anything were actually "immeasurable," it would bear no relationship of any kind to the rest of the universe, it would not affect nor be affected by anything else in any manner whatever, it would enact no causes and bear no consequences—in short, it would not exist.

The motive of the anti-measurement attitude is obvious: it is the desire to preserve a sanctuary of the indeterminate for the benefit of the irrational—the desire, epistemologically, to escape from the responsibility of cognitive precision and wide-scale integration; and, metaphysically, the desire to escape from the absolutism of existence, of facts, of reality and, above all, of *identity*.

5. Definitions

A definition is a statement that identifies the nature of the units subsumed under a concept.

It is often said that definitions state the meaning of words. This is true, but it is not exact. A word is merely a visual-auditory symbol used to represent a concept; a word has no meaning other than that of the concept it symbolizes, and the meaning of a concept consists of its units. It is not words, but concepts that man defines—by specifying their referents.

The purpose of a definition is to distinguish a concept from all other concepts and thus to keep its units differentiated from all other existents.

Since the definition of a concept is formulated in terms of other concepts, it enables man, not only to identify and *retain* a concept, but also to establish the relationships, the hierarchy, the *integration* of all his concepts and thus the integration of his knowledge. Definitions preserve, not the chronological order in which a given man may have learned concepts, but the *logical* order of their hierarchical interdependence.

With certain significant exceptions, every concept can be defined and communicated in terms of other concepts. The exceptions are concepts referring to sensations, and metaphysical axioms.

Sensations are the primary material of consciousness and, therefore, cannot be communicated by means of the material which is derived from them. The existential causes of sensations can be described and defined in conceptual terms (e.g., the wavelengths of light and the structure of the human eye, which produce the sensations of color), but one cannot communicate what color is like, to a person who is born blind. To define the meaning of the concept "blue," for instance, one must point to some blue objects to signify, in effect: "I mean *this*." Such an identification of a concept is known as an "ostensive definition."

Ostensive definitions are usually regarded as applicable only to conceptualized sensations. But they are applicable to axioms as well. Since axiomatic concepts are identifications of irreducible primaries, the only way to define one is by means of an ostensive definition—e.g., to define "existence," one would have to sweep one's arm around and say: "I mean *this*." (We shall discuss axioms later.)

The rules of correct definition are derived from the process of concept-formation. The units of a concept were differentiated—by means of a distinguishing characteristic(s)—from other existents possessing a commensurable characteristic, a Conceptual Common Denominator. A definition follows the same principle: it specifies the distinguishing characteristic(s) of the units, and indicates the category of existents from which they were differentiated.

The distinguishing characteristic(s) of the units becomes the *differentia* of the concept's definition; the existents possessing a Conceptual Common Denominator become the *genus*.

Thus a definition complies with the two essential functions of consciousness: differentiation and integration. The differentia isolates the units of a concept from all other existents; the genus indicates their connection to a wider group of existents.

For instance, in the definition of table ("An item of furniture, consisting of a flat, level surface and supports, intended to support other, smaller objects"), the specified shape is the differentia, which distinguishes tables from the other entities belonging to the same genus: furniture. In the definition of man ("A rational animal"), "rational" is the differentia, "animal" is the genus.

Just as a concept becomes a unit when integrated with others into a wider concept, so a genus becomes a single unit, a *species*, when integrated with others into a wider genus. For instance, "table" is a species of the genus "furniture," which is a species of the genus "household goods," which is a species of the genus "man-made objects." "Man" is a species of the genus "animal," which is a species of the genus "organism," which is a species of the genus "entity."

A definition is not a description; it *implies*, but does not mention all the characteristics of a concept's units. If a definition were to list all the characteristics, it would defeat its own purpose: it would provide an indiscriminate, undifferentiated and, in effect, pre-conceptual conglomeration of characteristics which would not serve to distinguish the units from all other existents, nor the concept from all other concepts. A definition must identify the *nature* of the units, i.e., the *essential* characteristics without which the units would not be the kind of existents they are. But it is important to remember that a definition implies *all* the characteristics of the units, since it identifies their *essential,* not their *exhaustive,* characteristics; since it designates *existents,* not their isolated aspects; and since it is a condensation of, not a substitute for, a wider knowledge of the existents involved.

This leads to a crucial question: since a group of existents may possess more than one characteristic distinguishing them from other existents, how does one determine the essential characteristic of an existent and, therefore, the proper defining characteristic of a concept?

The answer is provided by the process of concept-formation.

Concepts are not and cannot be formed in a vacuum; they are formed in a context; the process of conceptualization consists of observing the differences and similarities of the existents *within the field of one's awareness* (and organizing them into concepts accordingly). From a child's grasp of the simplest concept integrating a group of perceptually given concretes, to a scientist's grasp of the most complex abstractions integrating long conceptual chains—all conceptualization is a contextual process; the context is the entire field of a mind's awareness or knowledge at any level of its cognitive development.

This does not mean that conceptualization is a subjective process or that the content of concepts depends on an individual's subjective (i.e., arbitrary) choice. The only issue open to an individual's choice in this matter is how much knowledge he will seek to acquire and, consequently, what conceptual complexity he will be able to reach. But so long as and to the extent that his mind deals with concepts (as distinguished from memorized sounds and floating abstractions), the content of his concepts is determined and dictated by the cognitive content of his mind, i.e., by his grasp of the facts of reality. If his grasp is non-contradictory, then even if the scope of his knowledge is modest and the content of his concepts is primitive, *it will not contradict the content of the same concepts in the mind of the most advanced scientists.*

The same is true of definitions. *All definitions are contextual,* and a primitive definition *does not contradict* a more advanced one: the latter merely expands the former.

As an example, let us trace the development of the concept "man."

On the pre-verbal level of awareness, when a child first learns to differentiate men from the rest of his perceptual field, he observes distinguishing characteristics which, if translated into words, would amount to a definition such as: "A thing that moves and makes sounds." Within the context of his awareness, this is a valid definition:

man, in fact, does move and make sounds, and this distinguishes him from the inanimate objects around him.

When the child observes the existence of cats, dogs and automobiles, his definition ceases to be valid: it is still true that man moves and makes sounds, but these characteristics do not distinguish him from other entities in the field of the child's awareness. The child's (wordless) definition then changes to some equivalent of: "A living thing that walks on two legs and has no fur," with the characteristics of "moving and making sounds" remaining implicit, but no longer defining. Again, this definition is valid—within the context of the child's awareness.

When the child learns to speak and the field of his awareness expands still further, his definition of man expands accordingly. It becomes something like: "A living being that speaks and does things no other living beings can do."

This type of definition will suffice for a long time (a great many men, some modern scientists among them, never progress beyond some variant of this definition). But this ceases to be valid at about the time of the child's adolescence, when he observes (if his conceptual development continues) that his knowledge of the "things no other living beings can do" has grown to an enormous, incoherent, unexplained collection of activities, some of which are performed by all men, but some are not, some of which are even performed by animals (such as building shelters), but in some significantly different manner, etc. He realizes that his definition is neither applicable equally to all men, nor does it serve to distinguish men from all other living beings.

It is at this stage that he asks himself: What is the common characteristic of all of man's varied activities? What is their root? What capacity enables man to perform them and thus distinguishes him from all other animals? When he grasps that man's distinctive characteristic is his type of consciousness—a consciousness able to abstract, to form concepts, to apprehend reality by a process of reason—he reaches the one and only valid definition of man, within the context of his knowledge and of all of mankind's knowledge to date: *"A rational animal."*

("Rational," in this context, does not mean "acting invariably in accordance with reason"; it means "possessing the faculty of reason." A full biological definition of man would include many sub-categories of "animal," but the general category and the ultimate definition remain the same.)

Observe that all of the above versions of a definition of man were *true,* i.e., were correct identifications of the facts of reality—and that they were valid *qua* definitions, i.e., were correct selections of distinguishing characteristics in a given context of knowledge. None of them was contradicted by subsequent knowledge: they were included implicitly, as non-defining characteristics, in a more precise definition of man. It is still true that man is a rational animal who speaks, does things no other living beings can do, walks on two legs, has no fur, moves and makes sounds.

The specific steps given in this example are not necessarily the literal steps of the conceptual development of every man, there may be many more steps (or fewer), they may not be as clearly and consciously delimited—but this is the *pattern* of development which most concepts and definitions undergo in a man's mind with the growth of his knowledge. It is the pattern which makes intensive study and, therefore, the growth of knowledge—*and of science*—possible.

Now observe, on the above example, the process of determining an essential characteristic: the rule of *fundamentality*. When a given group of existents has more than one characteristic distinguishing it from other existents, man must observe the relationships among these various characteristics and discover the one on which all the others (or the greatest number of others) depend, i.e., the fundamental characteristic without which the others would not be possible. This fundamental characteristic is the *essential* distinguishing characteristic of the existents involved, and the proper *defining* characteristic of the concept.

Metaphysically, a fundamental characteristic is that distinctive characteristic which makes the greatest number of others possible; epistemologically, it is the one that explains the greatest number of others.

For instance, one could observe that man is the only animal who speaks English, wears wristwatches, flies airplanes, manufactures lipstick, studies geometry, reads newspapers, writes poems, darns socks, etc. None of these is an essential characteristic: none of them explains the others; none of them applies to all men; omit any or all of them, assume a man who has never done any of these things, and he will still be a *man*. But observe that all these activities (and innumerable others) require a *conceptual grasp* of reality, that an animal would not be able to understand them, that they are the expressions and consequences of man's rational faculty, that an organism without that faculty would *not* be a man—and you will know why man's rational faculty is his *essential* distinguishing and defining characteristic.

If definitions are contextual, how does one determine an objective definition valid for all men? It is determined according to the widest context of knowledge available to man on the subjects relevant to the units of a given concept.

Objective validity is determined by reference to the facts of reality. But it is man who has to identify the facts; objectivity requires discovery by man—and cannot precede man's knowledge, i.e., cannot require omniscience. Man *cannot* know more than he has discovered—and he *may not* know less than the evidence indicates, if his concepts and definitions are to be objectively valid.

In this issue, an ignorant adult is in the same position as a child or adolescent. He has to act within the scope of such knowledge as he possesses and of his correspondingly primitive conceptual definitions. When he moves into a wider field of action and thought, when new evidence confronts him, he has to expand his definitions according to the evidence, if they are to be objectively valid.

An objective definition, valid for all men, is one that designates the *essential* distinguishing characteristic(s) and genus of the existents subsumed under a given concept—according to all the relevant knowledge available at that stage of mankind's development.

(Who decides, in case of disagreements? As in all issues pertaining to objectivity, there is no ultimate authority, except reality and the mind of every individual who judges the evidence by the *objective* method of judgment: logic.)

This does not mean that every man has to be a universal scholar and that every discovery of science affects the definitions of concepts: when science discovers some previously unknown aspects of reality, it forms *new* concepts to identify them (e.g., "electron"); but insofar as science is concerned with the intensive study of previously known and conceptualized existents, its discoveries are identified by means of conceptual sub-categories. For instance, man is classified biologically in several sub-categories of "animal," such as "mammal," etc. But this does not alter the fact that rationality is his essential distinguishing and defining characteristic, and that "animal" is the wider genus to which he belongs. (And it does not alter the fact that when a scientist and an illiterate use the concept "man," they are referring to the same kind of entities.)

Only when and if some discovery were to make

the definition "rational animal" inaccurate (i.e., no longer serving to distinguish man from all other existents) would the question of expanding the definition arise. "Expanding" does not mean negating, abrogating or contradicting; it means demonstrating that some other characteristics are more distinctive of man than rationality and animality—in which unlikely case these two would be regarded as non-defining characteristics, but would still remain true.

Remember that concept-formation is a method of cognition, man's method, and that concepts represent classifications of observed existents according to their relationships to other observed existents. Since man is not omniscient, a definition cannot be changelessly absolute, because it cannot establish the relationship of a given group of existents to everything else in the universe, including the undiscovered and unknown. And for the very same reasons, a definition is false and worthless if it is not *contextually* absolute—if it does not specify the known relationships among existents (in terms of the known *essential* characteristics) or if it contradicts the known (by omission or evasion).

The nominalists of modern philosophy, particularly the logical positivists and linguistic analysts, claim that the alternative of true or false is not applicable to definitions, only to "factual" propositions. Since words, they claim, represent arbitrary human (social) conventions, and concepts have no objective referents in reality, a definition can be neither true nor false. The assault on reason has never reached a deeper level or a lower depth than this.

Propositions consist of words—and the question of how a series of sounds unrelated to the facts of reality can produce a "factual" proposition or establish a criterion of discrimination between truth and falsehood, is a question not worth debating. Nor can it be debated by means of inarticulate sounds that switch meanings at the whim of any speaker's mood, stupor or expediency of any given moment. (But the results of that notion can be observed in university classrooms, in the offices of psychiatrists, or on the front pages of today's newspapers.)

Truth is the product of the recognition (i.e., identification) of the facts of reality. Man identifies and integrates the facts of reality by means of concepts. He retains concepts in his mind by means of definitions. He organizes concepts into propositions—and the truth or falsehood of his propositions rests, not only on their relation to the facts he asserts, but also on the truth or falsehood of the definitions of the concepts he uses to assert them, which rests on the truth or falsehood of his designations of *essential* characteristics.

Every concept stands for a number of propositions. A concept identifying perceptual concretes stands for some implicit propositions; but on the higher levels of abstraction, a concept stands for chains and paragraphs and pages of *explicit* propositions referring to complex factual data. *A definition is the condensation of a vast body of observations—and stands or falls with the truth or falsehood of these observations.* Let me repeat: *a definition is a condensation.* As a legal preamble (referring here to *epistemological* law), every definition begins with the implicit proposition: "After full consideration of all the known facts pertaining to this group of existents, the following has been demonstrated to be their essential, therefore defining, characteristic . . ."

In the light of this fact, consider some modern examples of proposed definitions. A noted anthropologist, writing in a national magazine, suggests that man's essential distinction from all other animals, the essential characteristic responsible for his unique development and achievements, is the possession of a thumb. (The same article asserts that the dinosaur also possessed a thumb, but "somehow failed to develop.") What about man's type of consciousness? Blank out.

An article in a reputable encyclopedia suggests that man might be defined as "a language-having animal." Is "language-having" a primary characteristic, independent of any other characteristic or faculty? Does language consist of the ability to articulate sounds? If so, then parrots and mynabirds should be classified as men. If they should not, then what human faculty do they lack? Blank out.

There is no difference between such definitions and those chosen by individuals who define man as "a Christian (or Jewish or Mohammedan) animal" or "a white-skinned animal" or "an animal of exclusively Aryan descent," etc.—no difference in

epistemological principle or in practical consequences (or in psychological motive).

*The truth or falsehood of all of man's conclu-
sions, inferences, thought and knowledge rests on
the truth or falsehood of his definitions.*

(The above applies only to valid concepts.
There are such things as invalid concepts, i.e.,
words that represent attempts to integrate errors,
contradictions or false propositions, such as
concepts originating in mysticism—or words without specific definitions, without referents, which
can mean anything to anyone, such as modern
"anti-concepts." Invalid concepts appear occasion-
ally in men's languages, but are usually—though
not necessarily—short-lived, since they lead to cognitive dead-ends. An invalid concept invalidates
every proposition or process of thought in which it
is used as a cognitive assertion.)

Above the level of conceptualized sensations
and metaphysical axioms, every concept requires a
verbal definition. Paradoxically enough, it is the
simplest concepts that most people find it hardest
to define—the concepts of the perceptual concretes
with which they deal daily, such as "table,"
"house," "man," "walking," "tall," "number," etc.
There is a good reason for it: such concepts are,
chronologically, the first concepts man forms or
grasps, and can be defined verbally only by means
of later concepts—as, for instance, one grasps the
concept "table" long before one can grasp such
concepts as "flat," "level," "surface," "supports."
Most people, therefore, regard formal definitions
as unnecessary and treat simple concepts as if they

were pure sense data, to be identified by means of ostensive definitions, i.e., simply by pointing.

There is a certain psychological justification for this policy. Man's discriminated awareness begins with *percepts;* the conceptual identifications of daily-observed percepts have become so thoroughly automatized in men's minds that they seem to require no definitions—and men have no difficulty in identifying the referents of such concepts ostensively.

(This, incidentally, is one instance demonstrating the grotesque inversions of Linguistic Analysis: the stock-in-trade of linguistic analysts consists of reducing people to stammering helplessness by demanding that they define "house" or "which" or "but," then proclaiming that since people cannot define *even* such simple words, they cannot be expected to define more complex ones, and, therefore, there can be no such things as definitions—or concepts.)

In fact and in practice, so long as men *are* able to identify with full certainty the perceptual referents of simple concepts, it is not necessary for them to devise or memorize the verbal definitions of such concepts. What *is* necessary is a knowledge of the rules by which the definitions can be formulated; and what is *urgently* necessary is a clear grasp of that dividing line beyond which ostensive definitions are no longer sufficient. (That dividing line begins at the point where a man uses words with the feeling "I kinda know what I mean.") Most people have no grasp of that line and no inkling of the necessity to grasp it—and the disastrous, paralyzing, stultifying consequences are the greatest single cause of mankind's intellectual erosion.

(As an illustration, observe what Bertrand Russell was able to perpetrate because people thought they "kinda knew" the meaning of the concept "number"—and what the collectivists were able to perpetrate because people did not even pretend to know the meaning of the concept "man.")

To know the exact meaning of the concepts one is using, one must know their correct definitions, one must be able to retrace the specific (logical, not chronological) steps by which they were formed, and one must be able to demonstrate their connection to their base in perceptual reality.

When in doubt about the meaning or the definition of a concept, the best method of clarification is to look for its referents—i.e., to ask oneself: What fact or facts of reality gave rise to this concept? What distinguishes it from all other concepts?

For instance: what fact of reality gave rise to the concept "justice"? The fact that man must draw conclusions about the things, people and events around him, i.e., must judge and evaluate them. Is his judgment automatically right? No. What causes his judgment to be wrong? The lack of sufficient evidence, or his evasion of the evidence, or his inclusion of considerations other than the facts of the case. How, then, is he to arrive at the right judgment? By basing it exclusively on the factual evidence and by considering all the relevant evidence available. But isn't this a description of "objectivity"? Yes, "objective judgment" is one of the wider categories to which the concept "justice" belongs. What distinguishes "justice" from other instances of objective judgment? When one evaluates the nature or actions of inanimate objects, the criterion of judgment is determined by the particular purpose for which one evaluates them. But how does one determine a criterion for evaluating the character and actions of men, in view of the fact that men possess the faculty of volition? What science can provide an objective criterion of evaluation in regard to volitional matters? Ethics. Now, do I need a concept to designate the act of judging a man's character and/or actions exclusively on the basis of all the factual evidence available, and of evaluating it by means of an objective moral criterion? Yes. That concept is "justice."

Note what a long chain of considerations and observations is condensed into a single concept. And the chain is much longer than the abbreviated pattern presented here—because every concept used in this example stands for similar chains.

Please bear this example in mind. We shall discuss this issue further when we discuss the cognitive role of concepts.

Let us note, at this point, the radical difference between Aristotle's view of concepts and the Objectivist view, particularly in regard to the issue of essential characteristics.

It is Aristotle who first formulated the principles of correct definition. It is Aristotle who identified the fact that only concretes exist. But Aristotle held that definitions refer to metaphysical *essences,* which exist *in* concretes as a special element or formative power, and he held that the process of concept-formation depends on a kind of direct intuition by which man's mind grasps these essences and forms concepts accordingly.

Aristotle regarded "essence" as metaphysical; Objectivism regards it as *epistemological.*

Objectivism holds that the essence of a concept is that fundamental characteristic(s) of its units on which the greatest number of other characteristics depend, and which distinguishes these units from all other existents within the field of man's knowledge. Thus the essence of a concept is determined *contextually* and may be altered with the growth of man's knowledge. The metaphysical referent of man's concepts is not a special, separate metaphysical essence, but the *total* of the facts of reality he has observed, and this total determines which characteristics of a given group of existents he designates as *essential.* An essential characteristic is factual, in the sense that it does exist, does determine other characteristics and does distinguish a group of existents from all others; it is *epistemological* in the sense that the classification of "essential characteristic" is a device of man's method of cognition—a means of classifying, condensing and integrating an ever-growing body of knowledge.

Now refer to the four historical schools of thought on the issue of concepts, which I listed in the foreword to this work—and observe that the dichotomy of "intrinsic or subjective" has played havoc with this issue, as it has with every issue involving the relationship of consciousness to existence.

The extreme realist (Platonist) and the moderate realist (Aristotelian) schools of thought regard the referents of concepts as *intrinsic*, i.e., as "universals" inherent in things (either as archetypes or as metaphysical essences), as special existents unrelated to man's consciousness—to be perceived by man directly, like any other kind of concrete existents, but perceived by some non-sensory or extrasensory means.

The nominalist and the conceptualist schools regard concepts as *subjective*, i.e., as products of man's consciousness, unrelated to the facts of reality, as mere "names" or notions arbitrarily assigned to arbitrary groupings of concretes on the ground of vague, inexplicable resemblances.

The extreme realist school attempts, in effect, to preserve the primacy of existence (of reality) by dispensing with consciousness—i.e., by converting concepts into concrete existents and reducing consciousness to the perceptual level, i.e., to the automatic function of grasping percepts (by supernatural means, since no such percepts exist).

The extreme nominalist (contemporary) school attempts to establish the primacy of consciousness by dispensing with existence (with reality)—i.e., by denying the status of existents even to concretes and converting concepts into conglomerates of fantasy, constructed out of the debris of other, lesser fantasies, such as words without referents or incantations of sounds corresponding to nothing in an unknowable reality.

To compound the chaos: it must be noted that the Platonist school begins by accepting the primacy of consciousness, by reversing the relationship of consciousness to existence, by assuming that reality must conform to the content of consciousness, not the other way around—on the premise that the presence of any notion in man's mind proves the existence of a corresponding referent in reality. But the Platonist school still retains some vestige of respect for reality, if only in unstated motivation: it distorts reality into a mystical construct in order to extort its sanction and validate subjectivism. The nominalist school begins, with empiricist humility, by negating the power of consciousness to form any valid generalizations about existence—and ends up with a subjectivism that requires no sanction, a consciousness freed from the "tyranny" of reality.

None of these schools regards concepts as *objective,* i.e., as neither revealed nor invented, but as produced by man's consciousness in accordance with the facts of reality, as mental integrations of factual data computed by man—as the products of a cognitive method of classification whose processes must be performed by man, but whose content is dictated by reality.

It is as if, philosophically, mankind is still in the stage of transition which characterizes a child in the process of learning to speak—a child who is using his conceptual faculty, but has not developed it sufficiently to be able to examine it self-consciously and discover that what he is using is *reason.*

6. Axiomatic Concepts

Axioms are usually considered to be propositions identifying a fundamental, self-evident truth. But explicit propositions as such are not primaries: they are made of concepts. The base of man's knowledge—of all other concepts, all axioms, propositions and thought—consists of axiomatic concepts.

An axiomatic concept is the identification of a primary fact of reality, which cannot be analyzed, i.e., reduced to other facts or broken into component parts. It is implicit in all facts and in all knowledge. It is the fundamentally given and directly perceived or experienced, which requires no proof or explanation, but on which all proofs and explanations rest.

The first and primary axiomatic concepts are "existence," "identity" (which is a corollary of "existence") and "consciousness." One can study what exists and how consciousness functions; but one cannot analyze (or "prove") existence as such, or consciousness as such. These are irreducible primaries. (An attempt to "prove" them is self-contradictory: it is an attempt to "prove" existence by means of non-existence, and consciousness by means of unconsciousness.)

Existence, identity and consciousness are concepts in that they require identification in conceptual form. Their peculiarity lies in the fact that *they are perceived or experienced directly, but grasped conceptually*. They are implicit in every state of awareness, from the first sensation to the first percept to the sum of all concepts. After the first discriminated sensation (or percept), man's subsequent knowledge adds nothing to the basic facts designated by the terms "existence," "identity," "consciousness"—these facts are contained in any single state of awareness; but what *is* added by subsequent knowledge is *the epistemological need to identify them consciously and self-consciously*. The awareness of this need can be reached only at an advanced stage of conceptual development, when one has acquired a sufficient volume of knowledge—and the identification, the fully conscious grasp, can be achieved only by a process of abstraction.

It is not the abstraction of an attribute from a group of existents, but of a basic fact from all facts. Existence and identity are *not attributes* of existents, they *are* the existents. Consciousness is an attribute of certain living entities, but it is not an attribute of a given state of awareness, it *is* that state. Epistemologically, the formation of axiomatic concepts is an act of abstraction, a selective focusing on and mental isolation of metaphysical fundamentals; but metaphysically, it is an act of integration—*the widest integration possible to man:* it unites and embraces the total of his experience.

The units of the concepts "existence" and "identity" are every entity, attribute, action, event or phenomenon (including consciousness) that exists, has ever existed or will ever exist. The units of the concept "consciousness" are every state or process of awareness that one experiences, has ever experienced or will ever experience (as well as similar units, a similar faculty, which one infers in other living entities). The measurements omitted from axiomatic concepts are all the measurements of all the existents they subsume; what is retained, metaphysically, is only a fundamental fact; what is retained, epistemologically, is only one category of measurement, omitting its particulars: *time*—i.e., the fundamental fact is retained independent of any particular moment of awareness.

Axiomatic concepts are the *constants* of man's consciousness, the *cognitive integrators* that identify and thus protect its continuity. They identify explicitly the omission of psychological time measurements, which is implicit in all other concepts.

It must be remembered that conceptual awareness is the only type of awareness capable of integrating past, present and future. Sensations are merely an awareness of the present and cannot be retained beyond the immediate moment; percepts are retained and, through automatic memory, provide a certain rudimentary link to the past, but cannot project the future. It is only conceptual awareness that can grasp and hold the total of its experience—extrospectively, the continuity of existence; introspectively, the continuity of consciousness—and thus enable its possessor to project his course long-range. It is by means of axiomatic concepts that man grasps and holds this continuity, bringing it into his conscious awareness and *knowledge*. It is axiomatic concepts that identify the precondition of knowledge: the distinction between existence and consciousness, between reality and the awareness of reality, between the object and the subject of cognition. Axiomatic concepts are the foundation of *objectivity*.

Axiomatic concepts identify explicitly what is merely implicit in the consciousness of an infant or of an animal. (Implicit knowledge is passively held material which, to be grasped, requires a special focus and process of consciousness—a process which an infant learns to perform eventually, but which an animal's consciousness is unable to perform.)

If the state of an animal's perceptual awareness could be translated into words, it would amount to a disconnected succession of random moments such as "Here now table—here now tree—here now man—I now see—I now feel," etc.—with the next day or hour starting the succession all over again, with only a few strands of memory in the form of "This now food" or "This now master." What a man's consciousness does with the same material, by means of axiomatic concepts, is: "The table exists—the tree exists—man exists—I am conscious."

(The above projection of an animal's awareness

is what certain modern philosophers, such as logical positivists and logical atomists, ascribe to man, as his start and his only contact with reality—except that they reject the concept "reality," substitute sensations for percepts, and regard everything above this sub-animal level as an arbitrary human "construct.")

Since axiomatic concepts are not formed by differentiating one group of existents from others, but represent an integration of all existents, they have no Conceptual Common Denominator with anything else. They have no contraries, no alternatives. The contrary of the concept "table"—a non-table—is every other kind of existent. The contrary of the concept "man"—a non-man—is every other kind of existent. "Existence," "identity" and "consciousness" have no contraries—only a void.

It may be said that existence can be differentiated from non-existence; but non-existence is not a fact, it is the *absence* of a fact, it is a derivative concept pertaining to a relationship, i.e., a concept which can be formed or grasped only in relation to some existent that has ceased to exist. (One can arrive at the concept "absence" starting from the concept "presence," in regard to some particular existent(s); one cannot arrive at the concept "presence" starting from the concept "absence," with the absence including everything.) Non-existence as such is a zero with no sequence of numbers to follow it, it is the nothing, the total blank.

This gives us a lead to another special aspect of axiomatic concepts: although they designate a fundamental *metaphysical* fact, axiomatic concepts are the products of an *epistemological* need—the need of a volitional, conceptual consciousness which is capable of error and doubt. An animal's perceptual awareness does not need and could not grasp an equivalent of the concepts "existence," "identity" and "consciousness": it deals with them constantly, it is aware of existents, it recognizes various identities, but it takes them (and itself) as the given and can conceive of no alternative. It is only man's consciousness, a consciousness capable of conceptual errors, that needs a special identification of the directly given, to embrace and delimit the entire field of its awareness—to delimit it from the void of unreality to which conceptual errors can lead. Axiomatic concepts are epistemological guidelines. They sum up the essence of all human cognition: something *exists* of which I am *conscious;* I must discover its *identity.*

The concept "existence" does not indicate what existents it subsumes: it merely underscores the primary fact that they *exist.* The concept "identity" does not indicate the particular natures of the existents it subsumes; it merely underscores the primary fact that *they are what they are.* The concept "consciousness" does not indicate what existents one is conscious of: it merely underscores the primary fact that one is *conscious.*

This underscoring of primary facts is one of the crucial epistemological functions of axiomatic concepts. It is also the reason why they can be translated into a statement only in the form of a repetition (as a base and a reminder): Existence exists—Consciousness is conscious—A is A. (This converts axiomatic concepts into formal axioms.)

That special underscoring, which is of no concern to animals, is a matter of life or death for man—as witness, modern philosophy, which is a monument to the results of the attempt to evade or bypass such reminders.

Since axiomatic concepts refer to facts of reality and are not a matter of "faith" or of man's arbitrary choice, there is a way to ascertain whether a given concept is axiomatic or not: one ascertains it by observing the fact that an axiomatic concept cannot be escaped, that it is implicit in all knowledge, that it has to be accepted and used even in the process of any attempt to deny it.

For instance, when modern philosophers declare that axioms are a matter of arbitrary choice, and proceed to choose complex, derivative concepts as the alleged axioms of their alleged reasoning, one can observe that their statements imply and depend on "existence," "consciousness," "identity," which they profess to negate, but which are smuggled into their arguments in the form of unacknowledged, "stolen" concepts.

It is worth noting, at this point, that what the enemies of reason seem to know, but its alleged defenders have not discovered, is the fact that *axiomatic concepts are the guardians of man's mind and the foundation of reason*—the keystone, touchstone and hallmark of reason—and if reason is to be destroyed, it is axiomatic concepts that have to be destroyed.

Observe the fact that in the writings of every

school of mysticism and irrationalism, amidst all the ponderously unintelligible verbiage of obfuscations, rationalizations and equivocations (which include protestations of fidelity to reason, and claims to some "higher" form of rationality), one finds, sooner or later, a clear, simple, explicit denial of the validity (of the metaphysical or ontological status) of axiomatic concepts, most frequently of "identity." (For example, see the works of Kant and Hegel.) You do not have to guess, infer or interpret: they tell you. But what you do have to know is the full meaning, implications and consequences of such denials—which, in the history of philosophy, seem to be better understood by the enemies of reason than by its defenders.

One of the consequences (a vulgar variant of concept stealing, prevalent among avowed mystics and irrationalists) is a fallacy I call the *Reification of the Zero*. It consists of regarding "nothing" as a *thing*, as a special, different kind of *existent*. (For example, see Existentialism.) This fallacy breeds such symptoms as the notion that presence and absence, or being and non-being, are metaphysical forces of equal power, and that being is the absence of non-being. E.g., "Nothingness is prior to being." (Sartre) —"Human finitude is the presence of the *not* in the being of man." (William Barrett) —"Nothing is more real than nothing." (Samuel Beckett) —*"Das Nichts nichtet"* or "Nothing noughts." (Heidegger). "Consciousness, then, is not a stuff, but a *negation*. The subject is not a thing, but a *non*-thing. The subject carves its own world out of Being by means of negative determinations. Sartre describes consciousness as a 'noughting nought' *(néant néantisant)*. It is a form of being other than its own: a mode 'which has yet to be what it is, that is to say, which is what it is, that is to say, which is what it is not and which is not what it is.' " (Hector Hawton, *The Feast of Unreason,* London: Watts & Co., 1952, p. 162.)

(The motive? "Genuine utterances about the nothing must always remain unusual. It cannot be made common. It dissolves when it is placed in the cheap acid of mere logical acumen." Heidegger.)

A man's protestations of loyalty to reason are meaningless as such: "reason" is not an axiomatic, but a complex, derivative concept—and, particularly since Kant, the philosophical technique of concept stealing, of attempting to negate reason by means of reason, has become a general bromide, a gimmick worn transparently thin. Do you want to assess the rationality of a person, a theory or a philosophical system? Do not inquire about his or its stand on the validity of reason. Look for the stand on axiomatic concepts. It will tell the whole story.

7. The Cognitive Role of Concepts

The story of the following experiment was told in a university classroom by a professor of psychology. I cannot vouch for the validity of the specific numerical conclusions drawn from it, since I could not check it first-hand. But I shall cite it here, because it is the most illuminating way to illustrate a certain fundamental aspect of consciousness—of any consciousness, animal or human.

The experiment was conducted to ascertain the extent of the ability of birds to deal with numbers. A hidden observer watched the behavior of a flock of crows gathered in a clearing of the woods. When a man came into the clearing and went on into the woods, the crows hid in the tree tops and would not come out until he returned and left the way he had come. When three men went into the woods and only two returned, the crows would not come out: they waited until the third one had left. But when five men went into the woods and only four returned, the crows came out of hiding. Apparently, their power of discrimination did not extend beyond three units—and their perceptual-mathematical ability consisted of a sequence such as: one-two-three-many.

Whether this particular experiment is accurate or not, the truth of the principle it illustrates can be ascertained *introspectively:* if we omit all conceptual knowledge, including the ability to count in terms of numbers, and attempt to see how many units (or existents of a given kind) we can discriminate, remember and deal with by purely perceptual means (e.g., visually or auditorily, but *without counting*), we will discover that the range of man's *perceptual* ability may be greater, but not much greater, than that of the crow: we may grasp and hold five or six units at most.

This fact is the best demonstration of the cognitive role of concepts.

Since consciousness is a specific faculty, it has a specific nature or identity and, therefore, its range is limited: it cannot perceive everything at once; since awareness, on all its levels, requires an active process, it cannot do everything at once. Whether the units with which one deals are percepts or concepts, the range of what man can hold in the focus of his conscious awareness at any given moment, is limited. The essence, therefore, of man's incomparable cognitive power is the ability to reduce a vast amount of information to a minimal number of units—which is the task performed by his conceptual faculty. And the principle of *unit-economy* is one of that faculty's essential guiding principles.

Observe the operation of that principle in the field of mathematics. If the above described experiment were performed on a man, instead of on crows, he would be able to *count* and thus to remember a large number of men crossing the clearing (how large a number, would depend on the time available to perceive them all and to count).

A "number" is a mental symbol that integrates units into a single larger unit (or subdivides a unit into fractions) with reference to the basic number of "one," which is the basic mental symbol of "unit." Thus "5" stands for |||||. (Metaphysically, the referents of "5" are any five existents of a specified kind; epistemologically, they are represented by a single symbol.)

Counting is an automatized, lightning-like process of reducing the number of mental units one has to hold. In the process of counting—"one, two, three, four, etc."—a man's consciousness holds only one mental unit at any one moment, the particular mental unit that represents the sum he has identified in reality (without having to retain the perceptual image of the existents composing that sum). If he reaches, say, the sum of 25 (or 250), it is still a single unit, easy to remember and to deal with. But project the state of your own consciousness, if I now proceeded to give you that sum by means of perceptual units, thus: |||||||||| . . . etc.

Observe the principle of unit-economy in the structure of the decimal system, which demands of man's mind that it hold only ten symbols (including the zero) and one simple rule of notation for larger numbers or fractions. Observe the algebraic methods by which pages of complex calculations are reduced to a simple, single equation. Mathematics is a science of *method* (the science of measurement, i.e., of establishing quantitative relationships), a cognitive method that enables man to perform an unlimited series of integrations. Mathematics indicates the pattern of the cognitive role of concepts and the *psycho-epistemological* need they fulfill. Conceptualization is a *method* of expanding man's consciousness by reducing the number of its content's units—a systematic means to an unlimited integration of cognitive data.

A concept substitutes one symbol (one word) for the enormity of the perceptual aggregate of the concretes it subsumes. In order to perform its unit-reducing function, the symbol has to become automatized in a man's consciousness, i.e., the enormous sum of its referents must be instantly (implicitly) available to his conscious mind whenever he uses that concept, without the need of perceptual visualization or mental summarizing—in the same manner as the concept "5" does not require that he visualize five sticks every time he uses it.

For example, if a man has fully grasped the concept "justice," he does not need to recite to himself a long treatise on its meaning, while he listens to the evidence in a court case. The mere sentence "I must be just" holds that meaning in his mind automatically, and leaves his conscious attention free to grasp the evidence and to evaluate it according to a complex set of principles. (And, in case of doubt, the conscious recall of the precise meaning of "justice" provides him with the guidelines he needs.)

It is the principle of unit-economy that necessitates the definition of concepts in terms of *essential* characteristics. If, when in doubt, a man recalls a concept's definition, the essential characteristic(s) will give him an instantaneous grasp of the concept's meaning, i.e., of the nature of its referents. For example, if he is considering some social theory and recalls that "man is a rational animal," he will evaluate the validity of the theory accordingly; but if, instead, he recalls that "man is an animal possessing a thumb," his evaluation and conclusion will be quite different.

Learning to speak is a process of automatizing the use (i.e., the meaning and the application) of concepts. And more: all learning involves a process of automatizing, i.e., of first acquiring knowledge by fully conscious, focused attention and observation, then of establishing mental connections which make that knowledge automatic (instantly available as a context), thus freeing man's mind to pursue further, more complex knowledge.

The status of automatized knowledge in his mind is experienced by man as if it had the direct, effortless, self-evident quality (and certainty) of perceptual awareness. But it is *conceptual* knowledge—and its validity depends on the precision of his concepts, which require as strict a precision of meaning (i.e., as strict a knowledge of what specific referents they subsume) as the definitions of mathematical terms. (It is obvious what disasters will follow if one automatizes errors, contradictions and undefined approximations.)

This leads us to a crucial aspect of the cognitive role of concepts: *concepts represent condensations of knowledge,* which make further study and the division of cognitive labor possible.

Remember that the perceptual level of awareness is the base of man's conceptual development. Man forms concepts, as a system of classification, whenever the scope of perceptual data becomes too great for his mind to handle. Concepts stand for specific kinds of existents, including *all* the characteristics of these existents, observed and not-yet-observed, known and unknown.

It is crucially important to grasp the fact that a concept is an "open-end" classification which includes the yet-to-be-discovered characteristics of a given group of existents. All of man's knowledge rests on that fact.

The pattern is as follows: when a child grasps the concept "man," the knowledge represented by that concept in his mind consists of perceptual data, such as man's visual appearance, the sound of his voice, etc. When the child learns to differentiate between living entities and inanimate matter, he ascribes a new characteristic, "living," to the entity he designates as "man." When the child learns to differentiate among various types of consciousness, he includes a new characteristic in his concept of man, "rational"—and so on. The implicit principle guiding this process, is: "I know that there exists such an entity as man; I know many of his characteristics, but he has many others which I do not know and must discover." The same principle directs the study of every other kind of perceptually isolated and conceptualized existents.

The same principle directs the accumulation and transmission of mankind's knowledge. From a savage's knowledge of man, which was not much greater than a child's, to the present level, when roughly half the sciences (the humanities) are devoted to the study of man, the *concept* "man" has not changed: it refers to the same kind of entities. What has changed and grown is the knowledge of these entities. The definitions of concepts may change with the changes in the designation of essential characteristics, and conceptual reclassifications may occur with the growth of knowledge, but these changes are made possible by and do not alter the fact that a concept subsumes *all* the characteristics of its referents, including the yet-to-be-discovered.

Since concepts represent a system of cognitive classification, a given concept serves (speaking metaphorically) as a file folder in which man's mind files his knowledge of the existents it subsumes. The content of such folders varies from individual to individual, according to the degree of his knowledge—it ranges from the primitive, generalized information in the mind of a child or an illiterate to the enormously detailed sum in the mind of a scientist—but it pertains to the same referents, to the same kind of existents, and is subsumed under the same concept. This filing system makes possible such activities as learning, education, research—the accumulation, transmission and expansion of knowledge. (It is the epistemological obligation of every individual to know what his mental file contains in regard to any concept he uses, to keep it integrated with his other mental files, and to seek further information when he needs to check, correct or expand his knowledge.)

The extent of today's confusion about the nature of man's conceptual faculty, is eloquently demonstrated by the following: it is precisely the "open-end" character of concepts, the essence of their cognitive function, that modern philosophers cite in their attempts to demonstrate that concepts have no cognitive validity. *"When* can we claim that we know what a concept stands for?" they clamor—and offer, as an example of man's predicament, the fact that one may believe all swans to be white, then discover the existence of a black swan and thus find one's concept invalidated.

This view implies the unadmitted presupposition that concepts are not a cognitive device of man's type of consciousness, but a repository of closed, out-of-context omniscience—and that concepts refer, not to the existents of the external world, but to the frozen, arrested state of knowledge inside any given consciousness at any given moment. On such a premise, every advance of knowledge is a setback, a demonstration of man's ignorance. For example, the savages knew that man possesses a head, a torso, two legs and two arms; when the scientists of the Renaissance began to dissect corpses and discovered the nature of man's internal organs, they invalidated the savages' concept "man"; when modern scientists discovered that man possesses internal glands, they invalidated the Renaissance concept "man," etc.

Like a spoiled, disillusioned child, who had expected predigested capsules of automatic knowledge, a logical positivist stamps his foot at reality and cries that context, integration, mental effort and first-hand inquiry are too much to expect of him, that he rejects so demanding a method of cognition, and that he will manufacture his own "constructs" from now on. (This amounts, in effect, to the declaration: "Since the intrinsic has failed us, the subjective is our only alternative.") The joke is on his listeners: it is this exponent of a primordial mystic's craving for an effortless, rigid, automatic omniscience that modern men take for an advocate of a free-flowing, dynamic, *progressive* science.

It is the "open-end" character of concepts that permits the division of cognitive labor among men. A scientist could not specialize in a particular branch of study without a wider context, without the correlation and integration of his work to the other aspects of the same subject. Consider, for example, the science of medicine. If the concept "man" did not stand as the unifying concept of that science (if some scientists studied only man's lungs; others, only the stomach; still others, only the blood circulation; and still others, only the retina of the eye), if all new discoveries were not to be ascribed to the same entity and, therefore, were not to be integrated in strict com-

pliance with the law of non-contradiction, the collapse of medical science would not take long to
follow.

No single mind can hold all the knowledge
available to mankind today, let alone hold it in
minute detail. Yet that knowledge has to be integrated and has to be kept open to individual understanding and verification, if science is not to
collapse under the weight of uncorrelated, un-
proved, contradictory minutiae. Only the most rigorous epistemological precision can implement
and protect the advance of science. Only the strict-
est, contextually absolute definitions of concepts,
can enable men to integrate their knowledge, to
keep expanding their conceptual structure in
severely hierarchical order by forming new
concepts, when and as needed—and thus to condense information and to reduce the number of
mental units with which they have to deal.

Instead, men are taught, by the guardians of
scientific epistemology, the philosophers, that
conceptual precision is impossible, that integration is undesirable, that concepts have no factual referents, that a concept denotes nothing but
its defining characteristic, which represents nothing but an arbitrary social convention—and that a
scientist should take public polls to discover the
meaning of the concepts he uses. ("Don't look for
the meaning, look for the use.") The consequences
of such doctrines are becoming apparent in every
branch of science today, most obviously in the humanities.

Concepts represent a system of mental filing

and cross-filing, so complex that the largest electronic computer is a child's toy by comparison. This system serves as the context, the frame-of-reference, by means of which man grasps and classifies (and studies further) every existent he encounters and every aspect of reality. Language is the physical (visual-auditory) implementation of this system.

Concepts and, therefore, language are *primarily* a tool of cognition—*not* of communication, as is usually assumed. Communication is merely the consequence, not the cause nor the primary purpose of concept-formation—a crucial consequence, of invaluable importance to men, but still only a consequence. *Cognition precedes communication;* the necessary precondition of communication is that one have something to communicate. (This is true even of communication among animals, or of communication by grunts and growls among inarticulate men, let alone of communication by means of so complex and exacting a tool as language.) The primary purpose of concepts and of language is to provide man with a system of cognitive classification and organization, which enables him to acquire knowledge on an unlimited scale; this means: to keep order in man's mind and enable him to think.

Many kinds of existents are integrated into concepts and represented by special words, but many others are not and are identified only by means of verbal descriptions. What determines man's decision to integrate a given group of existents into a concept? The requirements of cognition (and the principle of unit-economy).

There is a great deal of latitude, on the periphery of man's conceptual vocabulary, a broad area where the choice is optional, but in regard to certain central categories of existents the formation of concepts is mandatory. This includes such categories as: (a) the perceptual concretes with which men deal daily, represented by the first level of abstractions; (b) new discoveries of science; (c) new man-made objects which differ in their essential characteristics from the previously known objects (e.g., "television"); (d) complex human relationships involving combinations of physical and psychological behavior (e.g., "marriage," "law," "justice").

These four categories represent existents with which men have to deal constantly, in many different contexts, from many different aspects, either in daily physical action or, more crucially, in mental action and further study. The mental weight of carrying these existents in one's head by means of perceptual images or lengthy verbal descriptions is such that no human mind could handle it. The need of condensation, of unit-reduction, is obvious in such cases.

For an example, I refer you to my brief analysis of the need to form the concept "justice" (in the chapter on "Definitions"). If that concept did not exist, *what number* of considerations would a man have to bear in mind simultaneously, at every step of the process of judging another man? Or if the concept "marriage" did not exist, what number of considerations would a man have to bear in mind and express, when proposing to a woman? (Ask yourself what that concept subsumes and condenses in your own mind.)

The descriptive complexity of a given group of existents, the frequency of their use, and the requirements of cognition (of further study) are the main reasons for the formation of new concepts. Of these reasons, the requirements of cognition are the paramount one.

The requirements of cognition forbid the arbitrary grouping of existents, both in regard to isolation and to integration. They forbid the random coining of special concepts to designate any and every group of existents with any possible combination of characteristics. For example, there is no concept to designate "Beautiful blondes with blue eyes, 5'5" tall and 24 years old." Such entities or groupings are identified *descriptively*. If such a special concept existed, it would lead to senseless duplication of cognitive effort (and to conceptual chaos): everything of significance discovered about that group would apply to all other young women as well. There would be no cognitive justification for such a concept—unless some *essential* characteristic were discovered, distinguishing such blondes from all other women and requiring special study, in which case a special concept would become necessary.

(This is the reason why such conceptual subdivisions as "dining table," "coffee table," etc. are not designated by special concepts, but are treated as qualified instances of the concept "table"—as mentioned in the chapter on "Abstraction from Abstractions.")

In the process of determining conceptual classification, neither the essential similarities nor the essential differences among existents may be ignored, evaded or omitted once they have been observed. Just as the requirements of cognition forbid the arbitrary subdivision of concepts, so they forbid the abitrary integration of concepts into a wider concept by means of obliterating their *essential* differences—which is an error (or falsification) proceeding from definitions by non-essentials. (This is the method involved in the obliteration of valid concepts by means of "anti-concepts.")

For example, if one took the capacity to run as man's essential characteristic and defined him as "a running animal," the next step would be the attempt to eliminate "non-essential" distinctions and to form a single, higher-level concept out of "running entities," such as a running man, a running river, a running stocking, a running movie, a running commentary, etc. (on some such grounds as the notion that entities have no epistemological priority over actions). The result would be cognitive stultification and epistemological disintegration.

Cognitively, such an attempt would produce nothing but a bad hash of equivocations, shoddy metaphors and unacknowledged "stolen" concepts. Epistemologically, it would produce the atrophy of the capacity to discriminate, and the panic of facing an immense, undifferentiated chaos of unintelligible data—which means: the retro-gression of an adult mind to the *perceptual* level of awareness, to the helpless terror of primitive man. (This is happening today in certain schools of biology and psychology, whose false definition of the concept "learning" has led to attempts to equate the "behavior" of a piece of magnetized iron with the "behavior" of man.)

The requirements of cognition determine the *objective* criteria of conceptualization. They can be summed up best in the form of an epistemolog-ical "razor": *concepts are not to be multiplied be-yond necessity*—the corollary of which is: *nor are they to be integrated in disregard of necessity.*

As to the optional area of concept-formation, it consists predominantly of subdivisions that denote subtle shades of meaning, such as adjectives which are almost, but not fully, synonymous. This area is the special province of literary artists: it represents a form of unit-economy that permits an enormous eloquence of expression (including emo-tional evocation). Most languages have words that have no single-word equivalent in other languages. But since words do have objective referents, such "optional" concepts of one language can be and are translated into another by means of descriptive phrases.

The optional area includes also the favorite category (and straw man) of modern philosophers: the "Borderline Case."

By "Borderline Case," they mean existents which share some characteristics with the referents of a given concept, but lack others; or which share some characteristics with the referents of two different concepts and are, in effect, epistemological middle-of-the-road'ers—e.g., certain primitive organisms that biologists are unable to classify fully as either animals or plants.

The modern philosophers' favorite examples of this "problem" are expressed by such questions as: "What precise shade of color represents the conceptual borderline between 'red' and 'orange'?" Or: "If you had never seen any swans but white ones, and then discovered a black one, by what criteria would you decide whether to classify it as a 'swan' or to give it a different name and coin a new concept?" Or: "If you discovered the existence of a Martian who had a rational mind, but a spider's body, would you classify him as a rational animal, i.e., as 'man'?"

All this is accompanied by the complaint that "Nature doesn't tell us which choice to make," and purports to demonstrate that concepts represent arbitrary groupings formed by human (social) whim, that they are not determined by objective criteria and have no cognitive validity.

What these doctrines do demonstrate is the failure to grasp the cognitive role of concepts—i.e., the fact that the requirements of cognition determine the objective criteria of concept-formation. The conceptual classification of newly discovered existents depends on the nature and extent of their differences from and similarities to the previously known existents.

In the case of black swans, it is objectively mandatory to classify them as "swans," because virtually all their characteristics are similar to the characteristics of the white swans, and the difference in color is of no cognitive significance. (Concepts are not to be multiplied beyond necessity.) In the case of the rational spider from Mars (if such a creature were possible), the differences between him and man would be so great that the study of one would scarcely apply to the other and, therefore, the formation of a new concept to designate the Martians would be objectively mandatory. (Concepts are not to be integrated in disregard of necessity.)

In the case of existents whose characteristics are equally balanced between the referents of two different concepts—such as primitive organisms, or the transitional shades of a color continuum—there is no cognitive necessity to classify them under either (or any) concept. The choice is optional: one may designate them as a sub-category of either concept, or (in the case of a continuum) one may draw approximate dividing lines (on the principle of "no more than x and no less than y"), or one may identify them *descriptively*—as the nominalists are doing when they present the "problem."

(This "problem" is a straw man, in the sense that it is a problem only to the traditional-realist theories of universals, which claim that concepts are determined by and refer to archetypes or metaphysical "essences.")

If it should be asked, at this point: Who, then, is to keep order in the organization of man's conceptual vocabulary, suggest the changes or expansions of definitions, formulate the principles of cognition and the criteria of science, protect the objectivity of methods and of communications within and among the special sciences, and provide the guidelines for the integration of mankind's knowledge?—the answer is: *philosophy*. These, precisely, are the tasks of epistemology. The highest responsibility of philosophers is to serve as the guardians and integrators of human knowledge.

This is the responsibility on which modern philosophy has not merely defaulted, but worse: which it has reversed. It has taken the lead in the disintegration and destruction of knowledge—and has all but committed suicide in the process.

Philosophy is the foundation of science; epistemology is the foundation of philosophy. It is with a new approach to epistemology that the rebirth of philosophy has to begin.

8. Consciousness and Identity

The organization of concepts into propositions, and the wider principles of language—as well as the further problems of epistemology—are outside the scope of this work, which is concerned only with the nature of concepts. But a few aspects of these issues must be indicated.

Since concepts, in the field of cognition, perform a function similar to that of numbers in the field of mathematics, the function of a proposition is similar to that of an equation: it applies conceptual abstractions to a specific problem.

A proposition, however, can perform this function only if the concepts of which it is composed have precisely defined meanings. If, in the field of mathematics, numbers had no fixed, firm values, if they were mere approximations determined by the mood of their users—so that "5," for instance, could mean five in some calculations, but six-and-a-half or four-and-three-quarters in others, according to the users' "convenience"—there would be no such thing as the science of mathematics.

Yet *this* is the manner in which most people use concepts, and are taught to do so.

Above the first-level abstractions of perceptual concretes, most people hold concepts as loose approximations, without firm definitions, clear meanings or specific referents; and the greater a concept's distance from the perceptual level, the vaguer its content. Starting from the mental habit of learning words without grasping their meanings, people find it impossible to grasp higher abstractions, and their conceptual development consists of condensing fog into fog into thicker fog—until the hierarchical structure of concepts breaks down in their minds, losing all ties to reality; and, as they lose the capacity to understand, their education becomes a process of memorizing and imitating. This process is encouraged and, at times, demanded by many modern teachers who purvey snatches of random, out-of-context information in undefined, unintelligible, contradictory terms.

The result is a mentality that treats the first-level abstractions, the concepts of physical exis-tents, as if they were percepts, and is unable to rise much further, unable to integrate new knowledge or to identify its own experience—a mentality that has not discovered the process of conceptualization in conscious terms, has not learned to adopt it as an active, continuous, self-initiated policy, and is left arrested on a concrete-bound level, dealing only with the given, with the concerns of the immediate moment, day or year, anxiously sensing an abyss of the unknowable on all sides.

To such mentalities, higher concepts are indeterminate splinters flickering in the abyss, which they seize and use at random, with a nameless sense of guilt, with the chronic terror of a dreadful avenger that appears in the form of the question: "What do you mean?"

Words, as such people use them, denote unidentified feelings, unadmitted motives, subconscious urges, chance associations, memorized sounds, ritualistic formulas, second-hand cues—all of it hung, like barnacles, on some swimming suggestion of some existential referent. Consequently (since one cannot form concepts of consciousness without reference to their existential content), the field of introspection, to such people, is an untouched jungle in which no conceptual paths have yet been cut. They are unable to distinguish thought from emotion, cognition from evaluation, observation from imagination, unable to discriminate between existence and consciousness, between object and subject, unable to identify the meaning of any inner state—and they spend their lives as cowed prisoners inside their own skulls, afraid to look out at reality, paralyzed by the mystery of their own consciousness.

These are the mentalities that modern philosophy now asks us to accept as the criterion of the meaning of concepts.

There is an element of grim irony in the emergence of Linguistic Analysis on the philosophical scene. The assault on man's conceptual faculty has been accelerating since Kant, widening the breach between man's mind and reality. The cognitive function of concepts was undercut by a series of grotesque devices—such, for instance, as the "analytic-synthetic" dichotomy which, by a route of tortuous circumlocutions and equivocations, leads to the dogma that a "necessarily" true proposition cannot be factual, and a factual proposition cannot be "necessarily" true. The crass skepticism and epistemological cynicism of Kant's influence have been seeping from the universities to the arts, the sciences, the industries, the legislatures, saturating our culture, decomposing language and thought. If ever there was a need for a Herculean philosophical effort to clean up the Kantian stables—particularly, to redeem language by establishing objective criteria of meaning and definition, which average men could not attempt—the time was *now*. As if sensing that need, Linguistic Analysis came on the scene for the avowed purpose of "clarifying" language—and proceeded to declare that the meaning of concepts is determined in the minds of average men, and that the job of philosophers consists of observing and reporting on how people use words.

The *reductio ad absurdum* of a long line of mini-Kantians, such as pragmatists and positivists, Linguistic Analysis holds that words are an arbitrary social product immune from any principles or standards, an irreducible primary not subject to inquiry about its origin or purpose—and that we can "dissolve" all philosophical problems by "clarifying" the use of these arbitrary, causeless, meaningless sounds which hold ultimate power over reality. (The implicit psychological confession is obvious: it is an attempt to formalize and elevate second-handedness into a philosophical vocation.)

Proceeding from the premise that words (concepts) are created by whim, Linguistic Analysis offers us a choice of whims: individual or collective. It declares that there are two kinds of definitions: "stipulative," which may be anything anyone chooses, and "reportive," which are ascertained by polls of popular use.

As reporters, linguistic analysts were accurate: Wittgenstein's theory that a concept refers to a conglomeration of things vaguely tied together by a "family resemblance" is a perfect description of the state of a mind out of focus.

Such is the current condition of philosophy. If, in recent decades, there has been an enormous "brain-drain" from the humanities, with the best minds seeking escape and *objective* knowledge in the physical sciences (as demonstrated by the dearth of great names or achievements in the humanities), one need look no further for its causes. The escape, however, is illusory. It is not the special sciences that teach man to think; it is philosophy that lays down the epistemological criteria of all special sciences.

To grasp and reclaim the power of philosophy, one must begin by grasping why concepts and definitions cannot and may not be arbitrary. To grasp that fully, one must begin by grasping the reason why man needs such a science as epistemology.

Man is neither infallible nor omniscient; if he were, a discipline such as epistemology—the theory of knowledge—would not be necessary nor possible: his knowledge would be automatic, unquestionable and total. But such is not man's nature. Man is a being of volitional consciousness: beyond the level of percepts—a level inadequate to the cognitive requirements of his survival—man has to acquire knowledge by his own effort, which he may exercise or not, and by a process of reason, which he may apply correctly or not. Nature gives him no automatic guarantee of his mental efficacy; he is capable of error, of evasion, of psychological distortion. He needs a *method* of cognition, which he himself has to discover: he must discover how to use his rational faculty, how to validate his conclusions, how to distinguish truth from falsehood, how to set the criteria of *what* he may accept as knowledge. Two questions are involved in his every conclusion, conviction, decision, choice or claim: *What* do I know?—and: *How* do I know it?

It is the task of epistemology to provide the answer to the "How?"—which then enables the special sciences to provide the answers to the "What?"

In the history of philosophy—with some very rare exceptions—epistemological theories have consisted of attempts to escape one or the other of the two fundamental questions which cannot be escaped. Men have been taught either that knowledge is impossible (skepticism) or that it is available without effort (mysticism). These two positions appear to be antagonists, but are, in fact, two variants on the same theme, two sides of the same fraudulent coin: the attempt to escape the responsibility of rational cognition and the absolutism of reality—the attempt to assert the primacy of consciousness over existence.

Although skepticism and mysticism are ultimately interchangeable, and the dominance of one always leads to the resurgence of the other, they differ in the form of their inner contradiction—the contradiction, in both cases, between their philosophical doctrine and their psychological motivation. Philosophically, the mystic is usually an exponent of the *intrinsic* (revealed) school of epistemology; the skeptic is usually an advocate of epistemological *subjectivism*. But, psychologically, the mystic is a subjectivist who uses intrinsicism as a means to claim the primacy of *his* consciousness over that of others. The skeptic is a disillusioned intrinsicist who, having failed to find automatic supernatural guidance, seeks a substitute in the collective subjectivism of others.

The motive of all the attacks on man's rational faculty—from any quarter, in any of the endless variations, under the verbal dust of all the murky volumes—is a single, hidden premise: the desire to exempt consciousness from the law of identity. The hallmark of a mystic is the savagely stubborn refusal to accept the fact that consciousness, like any other existent, possesses identity, that it is a faculty of a specific nature, functioning through specific means. While the advance of civilization has been eliminating one area of magic after another, the last stand of the believers in the miraculous consists of their frantic attempts to regard *identity* as the *disqualifying* element of consciousness.

The implicit, but unadmitted premise of the neo-mystics of modern philosophy, is the notion that only an ineffable consciousness can acquire a valid knowledge of reality, that "true" knowledge has to be causeless, i.e., acquired without any means of cognition.

The entire apparatus of Kant's system, like a hippopotamus engaged in belly-dancing, goes through its gyrations while resting on a single point: that man's knowledge is not valid because his consciousness possesses identity. "His argument, in essence, ran as follows: man is *limited* to a consciousness of a specific nature, which perceives by specific means and no others, therefore, his consciousness is not valid; man is blind, because he has eyes—deaf, because he has ears—deluded, because he has a mind—and the things he perceives do not exist, *because* he perceives them." (*For the New Intellectual.*)

This is a negation, not only of man's consciousness, but of *any* consciousness, of consciousness as such, whether man's, insect's or God's. (If one supposed the existence of God, the negation would still apply: either God perceives through no means whatever, in which case he possesses no identity—or he perceives by some divine means and no others, in which case his perception is not valid.) As Berkeley negated existence by claiming that "to be, is to be perceived," so Kant negates consciousness by implying that to be perceived, is not to be.

What Kant implied through coils of obfuscating verbiage, his more consistent followers declared explicitly. The following was written by a Kantian: "With him [Kant] all is phenomenal [mere appearance] which is relative, and all is relative which is an object to a conscious subject. The conceptions of the understanding as much depend on the constitution of our thinking faculties, as the perceptions of the senses do on the constitution of our intuitive faculties. Both *might* be different, were our mental constitution changed; both probably *are* different to beings differently constituted. The *real* thus becomes identical with the *absolute*, with the object as it is in itself, out of all relation to a subject; and, as all consciousness is a relation between subject and object, it follows that to attain a knowledge of the real we must go out of consciousness." (Henry Mansel, "On the Philosophy of Kant," reprinted in Henry Mansel, *Letters, Lectures and Reviews,* ed. H. W. Chandler, London: John Murray, 1873, p. 171.)

From primordial mysticism to this, its climax, the attack on man's consciousness and particularly on his conceptual faculty has rested on the unchallenged premise that any knowledge acquired by a *process* of consciousness is necessarily subjective and cannot correspond to the facts of reality, since it is "*processed* knowledge."

Make no mistake about the actual meaning of that premise: it is a revolt, not only against being conscious, but against being alive—since in fact, in reality, on earth, every aspect of being alive involves a process of self-sustaining and self-generated action. (This is an example of the fact that the revolt against identity is a revolt against existence. "The desire not to be anything, is the desire not to be." *Atlas Shrugged*.)

All knowledge *is* processed knowledge—whether on the sensory, perceptual or conceptual level. An "unprocessed" knowledge would be a knowledge acquired without means of cognition. Consciousness (as I said in the first sentence of this work) is not a passive state, but an active process. And more: the satisfaction of every need of a living organism requires an act of *processing* by that organism, be it the need of air, of food or of knowledge.

No one would argue (at least, not yet) that since man's body has to *process* the food he eats, no objective rules of proper nutrition can ever be discovered—that "true nutrition" has to consist of absorbing some ineffable substance without the participation of a digestive system, but since man is incapable of "true feeding," nutrition is a subjective matter open to his whim, and it is merely a social convention that forbids him to eat poisonous mushrooms.

No one would argue that since nature does not tell man automatically what to eat—as it does not tell him automatically how to form concepts—he should abandon the illusion that there is a right or wrong way of eating (or he should revert to the safety of the time when he did not have to "trust" objective evidence, but could rely on dietary laws prescribed by a supernatural power).

No one would argue that man eats bread rather than stones purely as a matter of "convenience."

It is time to grant to man's consciousness the same cognitive respect one grants to his body—i.e., the same *objectivity*.

Objectivity begins with the realization that man (including his every attribute and faculty, including his consciousness) is an entity of a specific nature who must act accordingly; that there is no escape from the law of identity, neither in the universe with which he deals nor in the working of his own consciousness, and if he is to acquire knowledge of the first, he must discover the proper method of using the second; that there is no room for the *arbitrary* in any activity of man, least of all in his method of cognition—and just as he has learned to be guided by objective criteria in making his physical tools, so he must be guided by objective criteria in forming his tools of cognition: his concepts.

Just as man's physical existence was liberated when he grasped the principle that "nature, to be commanded, must be obeyed," so his consciousness will be liberated when he grasps that *nature, to be apprehended, must be obeyed*—that the rules of cognition must be derived from the nature of existence and the nature, the *identity*, of his cognitive faculty.

Summary

1. Cognition and Measurement. The base of all of man's knowledge is the perceptual level of awareness. It is in the form of percepts that man grasps the evidence of his senses and apprehends reality. The building-block of man's knowledge is the concept of "existent" which is implicit in every percept. The (implicit) concept "existent" undergoes three stages of development in man's mind: *entity-identity-unit.* The ability to regard entities as units is man's distinctive method of cognition. A unit is an existent regarded as a separate member of a group of two or more similar members. Measurement is the identification of a quantitative relationship, by means of a standard that serves as a unit. The purpose of measurement is to expand the range of man's knowledge beyond the directly perceivable concretes.

2. Concept-Formation. Similarity is the relationship between two or more existents which possess the same characteristic(s), but in different measure or degree. The process of concept-formation consists of mentally isolating two or more existents by means of their distinguishing characteristic, and retaining this characteristic while omitting their particular measurements —on the principle that these measurements must exist in *some* quantity, but may exist in *any* quantity. A concept is a mental integration of two or more units possessing the same distinguishing characteristic(s), with their particular measurements omitted.

3. *Abstraction from Abstractions.* When concepts are integrated into a wider concept, they serve as units and are treated *epistemologically* as if each were a single (mental) concrete—always remembering that *metaphysically* (i.e., in reality) each unit stands for an unlimited number of concretes of a certain kind. When concepts are integrated into a wider one, the new concept includes *all* the characteristics of its constituent units; but their distinguishing characteristics are regarded as omitted measurements, and one of their common characteristics becomes the distinguishing characteristic of the new concept. When a concept is subdivided into narrower ones, its distinguishing characteristic is retained and is given a narrower range of specified measurements or is combined with an additional characteristic(s) to form the individual distinguishing characteristics of the new concepts.

4. *Concepts of Consciousness.* Every state of consciousness involves two fundamental attributes: the *content* (or object) of awareness, and the *action* (or process) of consciousness in regard to that content. A concept pertaining to consciousness is a mental integration of two or more instances of a psychological process possessing the same distinguishing characteristic(s), with the particular contents and the measurements of the action's intensity omitted. The intensity of a psychological process is measured on a comparative scale. Concepts pertaining to cognition are measured by the scope of their factual content and by the length of the conceptual chain required to grasp it. Concepts pertaining to evaluation are measured by

reference to a person's hierarchy of values; this involves a process of "teleological measurement" which deals, not with cardinal, but with *ordinal* numbers, establishing a graded relationship of means to ends, i.e., of actions to a standard of value. A special category of concepts of consciousness consists of concepts pertaining to the *products* of consciousness (e.g., "knowledge"), and concepts of *method* (e.g., "logic").

5. *Definitions.* A definition is a statement that identifies the nature of a concept's units. A correct definition must specify the distinguishing characteristic(s) of the units (the differentia), and indicate the category of existents from which they were differentiated (the genus). The *essential* distinguishing characteristic(s) of the units and the proper defining characteristic(s) of the concept must be a *fundamental* characteristic(s)—i.e., that distinctive characteristic(s) which, metaphysically, makes the greatest number of other distinctive characteristics possible and which, epistemologically, explains the greatest number of others. Just as the process of concept-formation is contextual, so *all definitions are contextual.* The designation of an essential characteristic depends on the context of man's knowledge; a primitive definition, if correct, does not contradict a more advanced one: the latter merely expands the former. An objective definition, valid for all men, is determined according to all the relevant knowledge available at that stage of mankind's development. Definitions are not changelessly absolute, but they are *contextually absolute.* A definition is false if it does not specify the known relationships among existents (in terms of the known *essential* characteristics) or if it contradicts the known. ·

Every concept stands for a number of implicit propositions. A definition is the *condensation* of a vast body of observations—and its validity depends on the truth or falsehood of these observations, as represented and summed up by the designation of a concept's essential, defining characteristic(s). The truth or falsehood of all of man's conclusions, inferences and knowledge rests on the truth or falsehood of his definitions. The radical difference between the Aristotelian view of concepts and the Objectivist view lies in the fact that Aristotle regarded "essence" as metaphysical; Objectivism regards it as epistemological.

6. Axiomatic Concepts. An axiomatic concept is the identification of a primary fact of reality, which is implicit in all facts and in all knowledge. It is perceived or experienced directly, but grasped conceptually. The first and primary axiomatic concepts are "existence," "identity" and "consciousness." They identify explicitly the omission of psychological time measurements, which is implicit in all concepts—and serve as constants, as cognitive integrators and epistemological guidelines. They embrace the entire field of man's awareness, delimiting it from the void of unreality to which conceptual errors can lead. Axiomatic concepts are not a matter of arbitrary choice; one ascertains whether a given concept is axiomatic or not by observing the fact that an axiomatic concept has to be accepted and used even in the process of any attempt to deny it. Axiomatic concepts are the foundation of objectivity.

7. The Cognitive Role of Concepts. The range of what man can hold in the focus of his conscious awareness at any given moment, is limited. The essence of his cognitive power is the ability to reduce a vast amount of information to a minimal number of units; this is the task performed by his conceptual faculty. Concepts represent condensations of knowledge, "open-

end" classifications that subsume *all* the characteristics of their referents, the known and the yet-to-be-
discovered; this permits further study and the division
of cognitive labor. The requirements of cognition
control the formation of new concepts, and forbid
arbitrary conceptual groupings. In the process of determining conceptual classifications, neither the essential differences nor the essential similarities among
existents may be ignored once they have been observed. To sum up in the form of an epistemological
"razor": *concepts are not to be multiplied beyond
necessity, nor are they to be integrated in disregard of
necessity.*

8. *Consciousness and Identity.* The assault on man's
conceptual faculty has been accelerating since Kant,
widening the breach between man's mind and reality.
To reclaim the power of philosophy, one must grasp
the reason why man needs epistemology. Since man is
neither infallible nor omniscient, he has to *discover* a
valid method of cognition. Two questions are involved
in his every conclusion or decision: *What* do I know?—
and: *How* do I know it? It is the task of epistemology
to provide the answer to the "How?"—which then enables the special sciences to provide the answer to the
"What?" In the history of philosophy, epistemological
theories have consisted predominantly of attempts to
escape one or the other of these two questions—by
means of skepticism or mysticism. The motive of all
the attacks on man's rational faculty, is a single basic
premise: the desire to exempt consciousness from the
law of identity. The implicit, but unadmitted premise
of modern philosophy is the notion that "true" knowledge must be acquired without any means of cognition,
and that identity is the *disqualifying* element of consciousness. This is the essence of Kant's doctrine,

which represents the negation of *any* consciousness, of consciousness as such. Objectivity begins with the realization that man (including his consciousness) is an entity of a specific nature who must act accordingly; that there is no escape from the law of identity; that there is no room for the arbitrary in any activity of man, least of all in his method of cognition—and that he must be guided by objective criteria in forming his tools of cognition: his concepts. Just as man's physical existence was liberated when he grasped that "nature, to be commanded, must be obeyed," so his consciousness will be liberated when he grasps that *nature, to be apprehended, must be obeyed*—that the rules of cognition must be derived from the nature of existence and the nature, the *identity*, of his cognitive faculty.

THE ANALYTIC-SYNTHETIC DICHOTOMY

by
Leonard Peikoff

Introduction

(This work was first published in
The Objectivist May–September 1967.)

Some years ago, I was defending capitalism in a discussion with a prominent professor of philosophy. In answer to his charge that capitalism leads to coercive monopolies, I explained that such monopolies are caused by government intervention in the economy and are logically impossible under capitalism. (For a discussion of this issue, see *Capitalism: The Unknown Ideal*.) The professor was singularly unmoved by my argument, replying, with a show of surprise and disdain:

"*Logically* impossible? Of course—granted your definitions. You're merely saying that, no matter what proportion of the market it controls, you won't call a business a 'coercive monopoly' if it occurs in a system you call 'capitalism.' Your view is true by arbitrary fiat, it's a matter of semantics, it's *logically* true but not *factually* true. Leave logic aside now; be serious and consider the actual empirical facts on this matter."

To the philosophically uninitiated, this response will be baffling. Yet they meet its equivalents everywhere today. The tenets underlying it permeate our intellectual atmosphere like the germs of an epistemological black plague waiting to infect and cut down any idea that claims the support of conclusive logical argumentation, a plague that spreads subjectivism and conceptual devastation in its wake.

This plague is a formal theory in technical philosophy; it is called: *the analytic-synthetic dichotomy*. It is accepted, in some form, by virtually every influential contemporary philosopher—pragmatist, logical positivist, analyst and existentialist alike.

The theory of the analytic-synthetic dichotomy penetrates every corner of our culture, reaching, directly or indirectly, into every human life, issue and concern. Its carriers are many, its forms subtly diverse, its basic causes complex and hidden—and its early symptoms prosaic and seemingly benign. But it is deadly.

The comparison to a plague is not, however, fully exact. A plague attacks man's body, not his conceptual faculty. And it is not launched by the profession paid to protect men from it.

Today, each man must be his own intellectual protector. In whatever guise the theory of the analytic-synthetic dichotomy confronts him, he must be able to detect it, to understand it, and to answer it. Only thus can he withstand the onslaught and remain epistemologically untouched.

The theory in question is not a philosophical primary; one's position on it, whether it be agreement or opposition, derives, in substantial part, from one's view of the nature of concepts. The Objectivist theory of concepts is presented above, in

Ayn Rand's *Introduction to Objectivist Epistemology*. In the present discussion, I shall build on this foundation. I shall summarize the theory of the analytic-synthetic dichotomy as it would be expounded by its contemporary advocates, and then answer it point by point.

The theory was originated, by implication, in the ancient world, with the views of Pythagoras and Plato, but it achieved real prominence and enduring influence only after its advocacy by such modern philosophers as Hobbes, Leibniz, Hume and Kant. (The theory was given its present name by Kant.) In its dominant contemporary form, the theory states that there is a fundamental cleavage in human knowledge, which divides propositions or truths into two mutually exclusive (and jointly exhaustive) types. These types differ, it is claimed, in their origins, their referents, their cognitive status, and the means by which they are validated. In particular, four central points of difference are alleged to distinguish the two types.

(a) Consider the following pairs of true propositions:

    i) A man is a rational animal.
    ii) A man has only two eyes.

    i) Ice is a solid.
    ii) Ice floats on water.

    i) 2 plus 2 equals 4.
    ii) 2 qts. of water mixed with 2 qts. of ethyl alcohol yield 3.86 qts. of liquid, at 15.56°C.

The *first* proposition in each of these pairs, it is said, can be validated *merely by an analysis of the meaning of its constituent concepts* (thus, these are called *"analytic"* truths). If one merely specifies the definitions of the relevant concepts in any of these propositions, and then applies the laws of logic, one can see that the truth of the proposition follows directly, and that to deny it would be to endorse a logical contradiction. Hence, these are also called "logical truths," meaning that they can be validated merely by correctly applying the laws of logic.

Thus, if one were to declare that "A man is *not* a rational animal," or that "2 plus 2 does *not* equal 4," one would be maintaining by implication that "A rational animal is *not* a rational animal," or that "1 plus 1 plus 1 plus 1, does *not* equal 1 plus 1 plus 1 plus 1"—both of which are self-contradictory. (The illustration presupposes that "rational animal" is the definition of "man.") A similar type of self-contradiction would occur if one denied that "Ice is a solid."

Analytic truths represent concrete instances of the Law of Identity; as such, they are also frequently called "tautologies" (which, etymologically, means that the proposition repeats "the same thing"; e.g., "A rational animal is a rational animal," The solid form of water is a solid"). Since all of the propositions of logic and mathematics can ultimately be analyzed and validated in this fashion, these two subjects, it is claimed, fall entirely within the "analytic" or "tautological" half of human knowledge.

Synthetic propositions, on the other hand—illustrated by the *second* proposition in each of the above pairs, and by most of the statements of daily life and of the sciences—are said to be entirely different on all these counts. A "synthetic" proposition is defined as one which *cannot* be validated merely by an analysis of the meanings or definitions of its constituent concepts. For instance, conceptual or definitional analysis alone, it is claimed, could not tell one whether ice floats on water, or what volume of liquid results when various quantities of water and ethyl alcohol are mixed.

In this type of case, said Kant, the predicate of the proposition (e.g., "floats on water") states something about the subject ("ice") which is not already contained in the meaning of the subject-concept. (The proposition represents a *synthesis* of the subject with a new predicate, hence the name.) Such truths cannot be validated merely by correctly applying the laws of logic; they do not represent concrete instances of the Law of Identity. To deny such truths is to maintain *a falsehood*, but *not a self-contradiction*. Thus, it is false to assert that "A man has three eyes," or that "Ice sinks in water"—but, it is said, these assertions are not self-contradictory. It is the *facts* of the case, not the laws of logic, which condemn such statements. Accordingly, synthetic truths are held to be "factual," as opposed to "logical" or "tautological" in character.

(b) Analytic truths are *necessary;* no matter what region of space or what period of time one considers, such propositions *must* hold true. Indeed, they are said to be true not only throughout the universe which actually exists, but in "all possible worlds"—to use Leibniz's famous phrase. Since its denial is self-contradictory, the opposite of any analytic truth is unimaginable and inconceivable. A visitor from an alien planet might relate many unexpected marvels, but his claims would be rejected out-of-hand if he announced that, in his world, ice was a gas, man was a postage stamp, and 2 plus 2 equaled 7.3.

Synthetic truths, however, are declared *not* to be necessary; they are called *"contingent."* This means: As a matter of fact, in the actual world that men now observe, such propositions *happen to be* true—but they do not *have to be* true. They are not true in "all possible worlds." Since its denial is not self-contradictory, the opposite of any synthetic truth is at least imaginable or conceivable. It is imaginable or conceivable that men should have an extra eye (or a baker's dozen of such eyes) in the back of their heads, or that ice should sink in water like a stone, etc. These things do not occur in our experience but, it is claimed, there is no logical necessity about this. The facts stated by synthetic truths are "brute" facts, which no amount of logic can make fully intelligible.

Can one conclusively *prove* a synthetic proposition? Can one ever be logically *certain* of its truth? The answer given is: "No. As a matter of logic, no synthetic proposition 'has to be' true; the opposite of any is conceivable." (The most uncompromising advocates of the analytic-synthetic dichotomy continue: "You cannot even be certain of the direct evidence of your senses—for instance, that you now see a patch of red before you. In classifying what you see as 'red,' you are implicitly declaring that it is similar in color to certain of your past experiences—and how do you know that you have remembered these latter correctly? That man's memory is reliable, is not a tautology; the opposite is conceivable.") Thus, the most one can ever claim for synthetic, contingent truths is some measure of probability; they are more-or-less-likely hypotheses.

(c) Since analytic propositions are "logically" true, they can, it is claimed, be validated *independently of experience;* they are "non-empirical" or "a priori" (today, these terms mean: "independent of experience"). Modern philosophers grant that some experience is required to enable a man to form concepts; their point is that, once the appropriate concepts have been formed (e.g., "ice," "solid," "water," etc.), no *further* experience is required to validate their combination into an analytically true proposition (e.g., "Ice is solid water"). The proposition follows simply from an analysis of definitions.

Synthetic truths, on the other hand, are said to be *dependent upon experience* for their validation; they are "empirical" or "a posteriori." Since they are "factual," one can discover their truth initially only by observing the appropriate facts directly or indirectly; and since they are "contingent," one can find out whether yesterday's synthetic truths are still holding today, only by scrutinizing the latest empirical data.

(d) Now we reach the climax: the characteristically twentieth-century *explanation* of the foregoing differences. It is: *Analytic propositions provide no information about reality, they do not describe facts, they are "non-ontological"* (i.e., do not pertain to reality). Analytic truths, it is held, are created and sustained by men's arbitrary decision to use words (or concepts) in a certain fashion, they merely record the implications of linguistic (or conceptual) *conventions*. This, it is claimed, is what accounts for the characteristics of analytic truths. They are non-empirical—because they say nothing about the world of experience. No fact can ever cast doubt upon them, they are immune from future correction—because they are immune from reality. They are necessary—because men make them so.

"The propositions of logic," said Wittgenstein in the *Tractatus,* "all say the same thing: that is, nothing." "The principles of logic and mathematics," said A. J. Ayer in *Language, Truth and Logic*, "are true universally simply because we never allow them to be anything else."

Synthetic propositions, on the other hand, *are* factual—and for this, man pays a price. The price is that they are contingent, uncertain and unprovable.

The theory of the analytic-synthetic dichotomy presents men with the following choice: If your statement is proved, it says nothing about that which exists; if it is about existents, it cannot be proved. If it is demonstrated by logical argument, it represents a subjective convention; if it asserts a fact, logic cannot establish it. If you validate it by an appeal to the meanings of your *concepts,* then it is cut off from reality; if you validate it by an appeal to your *percepts,* then you cannot be certain of it.

Objectivism rejects the theory of the analytic-synthetic dichotomy as false—in principle, at root, and in every one of its variants.

Now, let us analyze and answer this theory point by point.

"Analytic" and "Synthetic" Truths

An analytic proposition is defined as one which can be validated merely by an analysis of the meaning of its constituent concepts. The critical question is: *What is included in "the meaning of a concept"?* Does a concept mean the *existents* which it subsumes, including *all* their characteristics? Or does it mean only certain aspects of these existents, designating some of their characteristics but excluding others?

The latter viewpoint is fundamental to every version of the analytic-synthetic dichotomy. The advocates of this dichotomy divide the characteristics of the existents subsumed under a concept into two groups: those which are *included* in the meaning of the concept, and those—the great majority—which, they claim, are *excluded* from its meaning. The dichotomy among propositions follows directly. If a proposition links the "included" characteristics with the concept, it can be validated merely by an "analysis" of the concept; if it links the "excluded" characteristics with the concept, it represents an act of "synthesis."

For example: it is commonly held that, out of the vast number of man's characteristics (anatomical, physiological, psychological, etc.), *two*—"rationality" and "animality"—constitute the entire meaning of the *concept* "man." All the rest, it is held, are outside the concept's meaning. On this view, it is "analytic" to state that "A man is a rational animal" (the predicate is "included" in the subject-concept), but "synthetic" to state that "A man has only two eyes" (the predicate is "excluded").

The primary historical source of the theory that a concept includes some of an entity's characteristics, but excludes others, is the Platonic realist theory of universals. Platonism holds that concepts designate non-material essences (universals) subsisting in a supernatural dimension. Our world, Plato claimed, is only the reflection of these essences, in a material form. On this view, a physical entity possesses two very different types of characteristics: those which reflect its supernatural essence, and those which arise from the fact that, in this world, the essence is manifest in material form. The first are "essential" to the entity, and constitute its real nature; the second are matter-generated "accidents." Since concepts are said to designate essences, the concept of an entity includes its "essential" characteristics, but excludes its "accidents."

How does one differentiate "accidents" from "essential" characteristics in a particular case? The Platonists' ultimate answer is: By an act of "intuition."

(A more plausible and naturalistic variant of the essence-accident dichotomy is endorsed by Aristotelians; on this point, their theory of concepts reflects a strong Platonic influence.)

In the modern era, Platonic realism lost favor among philosophers; nominalism progressively became the dominant theory of concepts. The nominalists reject supernaturalism as unscientific, and the appeal to "intuition" as a thinly veiled subjectivism. They do not, however, reject the crucial consequence of Plato's theory: *the division of an entity's characteristics into two groups,* one of which is excluded from the concept designating the entity.

Denying that concepts have an objective basis in the facts of reality, nominalists declare that the source of concepts is a subjective human decision: men *arbitrarily* select certain characteristics to serve as the basis (the "essentials") for a classification; thereafter, they agree to apply the same term to any concretes that happen to exhibit these "essentials," no matter how diverse these concretes are in other respects. On this view, the concept (the term) means only those characteristics initially decreed to be "essential." The other characteristics of the subsumed concretes bear no necessary connection to the "essential" characteristics, and are excluded from the concept's meaning.

Observe that, while condemning Plato's *mystic* view of a concept's meaning, the nominalists embrace the same view in a *skeptic* version. Condemning the essence-accident dichotomy as implicitly arbitrary, they institute an *explicitly* arbitrary equivalent. Condemning Plato's "intuitive" selection of essences as a disguised subjectivism, they spurn the disguise and adopt subjectivism as their official theory—as though a concealed vice were heinous, but a brazenly flaunted one, rational. Condemning Plato's supernaturally determined essences, they declare that essences are *socially* determined, thus transferring to the province of *human whim* what had once been the prerogative of Plato's divine realm. The nominalists' "advance" over Plato consisted of *secularizing* his theory. To secularize an error is still to commit it.

Its form, however, changes. Nominalists do not say that a concept designates only an entity's "essence," excluding its "accidents." Their secularized version is: A concept is only a shorthand tag for the characteristics stated in its definition; a concept and its definition are interchangeable; *a concept means only its definition.*

It is the Platonic-nominalist approach to concept-formation, expressed in such views as these, that gives rise to the theory of the analytic-synthetic dichotomy. Yet its advocates commonly advance the dichotomy as a self-contained primary, independent of any particular theory of concepts. Indeed, they usually insist that the issue of concept-formation—since it is "empirical," not "logical"—is outside the province of philosophy. (!) (Thus, they use the dichotomy to discredit in advance any inquiry into the issues on which the dichotomy itself depends.)

In spite of this, however, they continue to advocate "conceptual analysis," and to distinguish which truths can—or cannot—be validated by its practice. One is expected to analyze concepts, without a knowledge of their source and nature—to determine their meaning, while ignorant of their relationship to concretes. How? The answer implicit in contemporary philosophical practice is: "Since people have already given concepts their meanings, we need only study common usage." In other words, paraphrasing Galt: "The concepts are here. How did they get here? Somehow." (*Atlas Shrugged.*)

Since concepts are complex products of man's consciousness, any theory or approach which implies that they are irreducible primaries, is invalidated by that fact alone. Without a theory of concepts as a foundation, one cannot, in reason, adopt *any* theory about the nature or kinds of propositions; propositions are only combinations of concepts.

The Objectivist theory of concepts undercuts the theory of the analytic-synthetic dichotomy at its root.

According to Objectivism, concepts "represent classifications of observed existents according to their relationships to other observed existents."

(Ayn Rand, *Introduction to Objectivist Epistemology;* all further quotations in this section, unless otherwise identified, are from this work.) To form a concept, one mentally *isolates* a group of concretes (of distinct perceptual units), on the basis of observed similarities which distinguish them from all other known concretes (similarity is "the relationship between two or more existents which possess the same characteristic(s), but in different measure or degree"); then, by a process of omitting the particular measurements of these concretes, one *integrates* them into a single new mental unit: the concept, which subsumes all concretes of this kind (a potentially unlimited number). The integration is completed and retained by the selection of a perceptual symbol (a word) to designate it. "A concept is a mental integration of two or more units possessing the same distinguishing characteristic(s), with their particular measurements omitted."

By isolating and integrating perceived concretes, by reducing the number of mental units with which he has to deal, man is able to break up and organize his perceptual field, to engage in specialized study, and to retain an unlimited amount of information pertaining to an unlimited number of concretes. Conceptualization is a method of acquiring and retaining knowledge of that which exists, on a scale inaccessible to the perceptual level of consciousness.

Since a word is a symbol for a concept, it has no meaning apart from the content of the concept it symbolizes. And since a concept is an integration of units, *it* has no content or meaning apart from its units. *The meaning of a concept consists of the units—the existents—which it integrates, including all the characteristics of these units.*

Observe that concepts mean *existents,* not arbitrarily selected portions of existents. There is no basis whatever—neither metaphysical nor epistemological, neither in the nature of reality nor of a conceptual consciousness—for a division of the characteristics of a concept's units into two groups, one of which is excluded from the concept's meaning.

Metaphysically, an entity is: all of the things which it is. Each of its characteristics has the same metaphysical status: each constitutes a part of the entity's identity.

Epistemologically, all the characteristics of the entities subsumed under a concept are discovered by the same basic method: by observation of these entities. The initial similarities, on the basis of which certain concretes were isolated and conceptually integrated, were grasped by a process of observation; all subsequently discovered characteristics of these concretes are discovered by the same method (no matter how complex the inductive procedures involved may become).

The fact that certain characteristics are, at a given time, *unknown* to man, does not indicate that these characteristics are excluded from the entity—*or from the concept.* A is A; existents are what they are, independent of the state of human knowledge; and a concept means the existents which it integrates. Thus, a concept subsumes and includes *all* the characteristics of its referents, known and not-yet-known.

(This does not mean that man is omniscient, or that he can capriciously ascribe any characteristics he chooses to the referents of his concepts. In order to discover that an entity possesses a certain characteristic, one must engage in a process of scientific study, observation and validation. Only then does one know that that characteristic is true of the entity and, therefore, is subsumed under the concept.)

"It is crucially important to grasp the fact that a concept is an 'open-end' classification which includes the yet-to-be-discovered characteristics of a given group of existents. All of man's knowledge rests on that fact.

"The pattern is as follows: When a child grasps the concept 'man,' the knowledge represented by that concept in his mind consists of perceptual data, such as man's visual appearance, the sound of his voice, etc. When the child learns to differentiate between living entities and inanimate matter, he ascribes a new characteristic, 'living,' to the entity he designates as 'man.' When the child learns to differentiate among various types of consciousness, he includes a new characteristic in his concept of man, 'rational'—and so on. The implicit principle guiding this process, is: 'I know that there exists such an entity as man; I know many of his characteristics, but he has many others which I do not know and must discover.' The same principle directs the study of every other kind of perceptually isolated and conceptualized existents.

"The same principle directs the accumulation and transmission of mankind's knowledge. From a savage's knowledge of man . . . [to the present level], the *concept* 'man' has not changed: it refers to the same kind of entities. What has changed and grown is the knowledge of these entities."

What, then, is the meaning of the concept "man"? "Man" means a certain type of entity, a rational animal, including *all* the characteristics of this entity (anatomical, physiological, psychological, etc., as well as the relations of these characteristics to those of other entities)—all the characteristics already known, and all those ever to be discovered. Whatever is true of the entity, is meant by the concept.

It follows that there are no grounds on which to distinguish "analytic" from "synthetic" propositions. Whether one states that "A man is a rational animal," or that "A man has only two eyes"—in both cases, the predicated characteristics are true of man and are, therefore, included in the concept "man." The meaning of the first statement is: "A certain type of entity, including all its characteristics (among which are rationality and animality) is: a rational animal." The meaning of the second is: "A certain type of entity, including all its characteristics (among which is the possession of only two eyes) has: only two eyes." Each of these statements is an instance of the Law of Identity; each is a "tautology"; to deny either is to contradict the meaning of the concept "man," and thus to endorse a self-contradiction.

A similar type of analysis is applicable to *every*

true statement. Every truth about a given existent(s) reduces, in basic pattern, to: "X is: one or more of the things which it is." The predicate in such a case states some characteristic(s) of the subject; but since it *is* a characteristic of the subject, the *concept(s)* designating the subject in fact includes the predicate from the outset. If one wishes to use the term "tautology" in this context, then *all* truths are "tautological." (And, by the same reasoning, all falsehoods are self-contradictions.)

When making a statement about an existent, one has, ultimately, only two alternatives: "X (which means X, the existent, including all its characteristics) *is* what it is"—or: "X *is not* what it is." The choice between truth and falsehood is the choice between "tautology" (in the sense explained) and self-contradiction.

In the realm of propositions, there is only one basic epistemological distinction: *truth vs. falsehood*, and only one fundamental issue: By what method is truth discovered and validated? To plant a dichotomy at the base of human knowledge—to claim that there are opposite *methods* of validation and opposite *types* of truth—is a procedure without grounds or justification.

In one sense, *no* truths are "analytic." No proposition can be validated merely by "conceptual analysis"; the content of the concept—i.e., the characteristics of the existents it integrates—must be discovered and validated by observation, before any "analysis" is possible. In another sense, *all* truths are "analytic." When some characteristic of an entity *has* been discovered, the proposition ascribing it to the entity will be seen to be "logically true" (its opposite would contradict the meaning of the concept designating the entity). In either case, the analytic-logical-tautological vs. synthetic-factual dichotomy collapses.

To justify their view that some of an entity's characteristics are excluded from the concept designating it, both Platonists and nominalists appeal to the distinction between the "essential" and the "non-essential" characteristics of an entity. For the Platonists, this distinction represents a *metaphysical* division, *intrinsic* to the entity, independent of man and of man's knowledge. For the nominalists, it represents a *subjective* human decree, independent of the facts of reality. For both schools, whatever their terminological or other differences, a concept means only the essential (or defining) characteristics of its units.

Neither school provides an *objective* basis for the distinction between an entity's "essential" and "non-essential" characteristics. (Supernaturalism—in its avowed or secularized form—is not an objective basis for anything.) Neither school explains why such a distinction is objectively required in the process of conceptualization.

This explanation is provided by Objectivism, and exposes the basic error in the Platonic-nominalist position.

When a man reaches a certain level of conceptual complexity, he needs to discover a method of organizing and interrelating his concepts; he needs a method that will enable him to keep each of his concepts clearly distinguished from all the others, each connected to a specific group of existents clearly distinguished from the other existents he knows. (In the early stages of conceptual development, when a child's concepts are comparatively few in number and designate directly perceivable concretes, "ostensive definitions" are sufficient for this purpose.) The method consists of *defining* each concept, by specifying the characteristic(s) of its units upon which the greatest number of their other known characteristics depends, and which distinguishes the units from all other known existents. The characteristic(s) which fulfills this requirement is designated the *"essential"* characteristic, in that context of knowledge.

Essential characteristics are determined contextually. The characteristic(s) which most fundamentally distinguishes a certain type of entity from all other existents known at the time, may not do so within a wider field of knowledge, when more existents become known and/or more of the entity's characteristics are discovered. The characteristic(s) designated as "essential"—and the definition which expresses it—may alter as one's cognitive context expands. Thus, essences are not intrinsic to entities, in the Platonic (or Aristotelian) manner; they are epistemological, not metaphysical. A definition in terms of essential characteristics "is a device of man's method of cognition—a means of classifying, condensing and integrating an ever-growing body of knowledge."

Nor is the designation of essential characteristics a matter of arbitrary choice or subjective decree. A contextual definition can be formulated only after one has fully considered *all* the known facts pertaining to the units in question: their similarities, their differences from other existents, the causal relationships among their characteristics, etc. This knowledge determines which characteristic(s) is *objectively* essential—and therefore, which definition is objectively correct—in a given cognitive context. Although the definition explicitly mentions only the essential characteristic(s), it implies and condenses all of this knowledge.

On the objective, contextual view of essences, a concept does *not* mean only the essential or defining characteristics of its units. To designate a certain characteristic as "essential" or "defining" is to *select,* from the total content of the concept, the characteristic that best condenses and differentiates that content in a specific cognitive context. Such a selection presupposes the relationship between the concept and its units: it presupposes that the concept is an integration of units, and that its content consists of its units, including *all* their characteristics. It is only because of this fact that the same concept can receive varying definitions in varying cognitive contexts.

When "rational animal" is selected as the definition of "man," this does not mean that the concept "man" becomes a shorthand tag for "anything whatever that has rationality and animality." It does not mean that the concept "man" is interchangeable with the phrase "rational animal," and that all of man's other characteristics are excluded from the concept. It means: A certain type of entity, including all its characteristics, is, in the present context of knowledge, most fundamentally distinguished from all other entities by the fact that it is a rational animal. All the presently available knowledge of man's *other* characteristics is required to validate this definition, and is implied by it. All these other characteristics remain part of the content of the concept "man."

The nominalist view that a concept is merely a shorthand tag for its definition, represents a profound failure to grasp the function of a definition in the process of concept-formation. The penalty for this failure is that the process of definition, in the hands of the nominalists, achieves the exact opposite of its actual purpose. The purpose of a definition is to keep a concept distinct from all others, *to keep it connected to a specific group of existents*. On the nominalist view, it is precisely this connection that is severed: as soon as a concept is defined, it ceases to designate *existents*, and designates instead only the defining characteristic.

And further: On a rational view of definitions, a definition organizes and condenses—and thus helps one to retain—a wealth of knowledge about the characteristics of a concept's units. On the nominalist view, it is precisely this knowledge that is *discarded* when one defines a concept: as soon as a defining characteristic is chosen, all the other characteristics of the units are banished from the concept, which shrivels to mean merely the definition. For instance, as long as a child's concept of "man" is retained ostensively, the child knows that man has a head, two eyes, two arms, etc.; on the nominalist view, as soon as the child defines "man," he discards all this knowledge; thereafter, "man" means to him only: "a thing with rationality and animality."

On the nominalist view, the process of defining a concept is a process of cutting the concept off from its referents, and of systematically evading what one knows about their characteristics. Definition, the very tool which is designed to promote conceptual integration, becomes an agent of its destruction, a means of *disintegration*.

The advocates of the view that a concept means its definition, cannot escape the knowledge that people actually use concepts to designate *existents*. (When a woman says: "I married a wonderful man," it is clear to most philosophers that she does not mean: "I married a wonderful combination of rationality and animality.") Having severed the connection between a concept and its referents, such philosophers sense that somehow this connection nevertheless exists and is important. To account for it, they appeal to a theory which goes back many centuries and is now commonly regarded as uncontroversial: the theory that a concept has *two kinds or dimensions* of meaning. Traditionally, these are referred to as a concept's *"extension"* (or "denotation") and its *"intension"* (or "connotation").

By the "extension" of a concept, the theory's advocates mean the concretes subsumed under that concept. By the "intension" of a concept, they mean those characteristics of the concretes which are stated in the concept's definition. (Today, this is commonly called the "conventional" intension; the distinction among various types of intension, however, merely compounds the errors of the theory, and is irrelevant in this context.) Thus, in the extensional sense, "man" means Socrates, Plato, Aristotle, Tom, Dick, Harry, etc. In the intensional sense, "man" means "rational animal."

A standard logic text summarizes the theory as follows: "The intension of a term, as we have noted, is what is usually called its definition. The extension, on the other hand, simply refers us to the set of objects to which the definition applies. . . . Extension and intension are thus intimately related, but they refer to objects in different ways—extension to a listing of the individuals who fall within its quantitative scope, intension to the qualities or characteristics of the individuals." (Lionel Ruby, *Logic: An Introduction.*)

This theory introduces another artificial split: between an existent and its characteristics. In the sense in which a concept means its referents (its extensional meaning), it does not mean or refer to their characteristics (its intensional meaning), and vice versa. One's choice, in effect, is: either to mean existents, apart from their characteristics—or (certain) characteristics, apart from the existents which possess them.

In fact, neither of these alleged types of meaning is metaphysically or epistemologically possible.

A concept cannot mean existents, apart from their characteristics. A thing is—what it is; its characteristics constitute its identity. An existent apart from its characteristics, would be an existent apart from its identity, which means: a nothing, a nonexistent. To be conscious of an existent *is* to be conscious of (some of) its characteristics. This is true on all levels of consciousness, but it is particularly obvious on the conceptual level. When one conceptualizes a group of existents, one isolates them mentally from others, *on the basis of certain of their characteristics*. A concept cannot integrate—or mean—a miscellaneous grab bag of objects; it can only integrate, designate, refer to and *mean*: existents of a certain kind, existents possessing certain characteristics.

Nor can the concept of an existent mean its characteristics (some or all), part from the existent which possesses them. A characteristic is an aspect of an existent. It is not a disembodied, Platonic universal. Just as a concept cannot mean existents apart from their identity, so it cannot mean identities apart from that which exists. Existence *is* Identity (*Atlas Shrugged*).

The theory that a concept means its definition, is not improved when it is combined with the view that, in another sense, a concept means its "extension." Two errors do not make a truth. They merely produce greater chaos and confusion. The truth is that a concept means the existents it integrates, including all their characteristics. It is this view of a concept's meaning that keeps man's concepts anchored to reality. On this view, the dichotomy between "analytic" and "synthetic" propositions cannot arise.

Necessity and Contingency

The theory of the analytic-synthetic dichotomy has its roots in two types of error: one epistemological, the other metaphysical. The epistemological error, as I have discussed, is an incorrect view of the nature of concepts. The metaphysical error is: the dichotomy between necessary and contingent facts.

This theory goes back to Greek philosophy, and was endorsed in some form by virtually all philosophical traditions prior to Kant. In the form in which it is here relevant, the theory holds that some facts are inherent in the nature of reality; they *must* exist; they are "necessary." Other facts, however, *happen to* exist in the world that men now observe, but they did not *have to* exist; they could have been otherwise; they are "contingent." For instance, that water is wet, would be a "necessary" fact; that water turns to ice at a certain temperature, would be "contingent."

Given this dichotomy, the question arises: How does one know, in a particular case, that a certain fact is necessary? Observation, it was commonly said, is insufficient for this purpose. "Experience," wrote Kant in the *Critique of Pure Reason*, "tells us, indeed, what is, but not that it must necessarily be so, and not otherwise." To establish that something is a fact, one employs observation and the appropriate inductive procedures; but, it was claimed, to establish that something is a fact is not yet to show that the fact in question is necessary. Some warrant or guarantee, over and above the fact's existence, is required if the fact is to be necessary; and some insight, over and above that yielded by observation and induction, is required to grasp this guarantee.

In the pre-Kantian era, it was common to appeal to some form of "intellectual intuition" for this purpose. In some cases, it was said, one could just "see" that a certain fact was necessary. *How* one could see this remained a mystery. It appeared that human beings had a strange, inexplicable capacity to grasp by unspecified means that certain facts not only were, but had to be. In other cases, no such intuition operated, and the facts in question were deemed contingent.

In the post-Kantian era, appeals to "intellectual intuition" lost favor among philosophers, but the necessary-contingent dichotomy went on. Perpetuated in various forms in the nineteenth century, it was reinterpreted in the twentieth as follows: since facts are learned only by experience, and experience does not reveal necessity, the concept of "necessary facts" must be abandoned. Facts, it is now held, are one and all contingent—and the propositions describing them are "contingent truths." As for necessary truths, they are merely the products of man's linguistic or conceptual conventions. They do not refer to facts, they are empty, "analytic," "tautological." In this manner, the necessary-contingent dichotomy is used to support the alleged distinction between analytic and synthetic propositions. Today, it is a commonplace for philosophers to remark that "factual" statements are "synthetic" and "contingent," whereas "necessary" statements are "non-factual" and "analytic."

(Contemporary philosophers prefer to talk about propositions or statements, rather than about facts; they rarely say that *facts* are contingent, attributing contingency instead to *statements* about facts. There is nothing to justify this mode of speech, and I shall not adhere to it in discussing their views.)

Observe that both the traditional pre-Kantians, and the contemporary conventionalists, are in essential agreement: both endorse the necessary-contingent dichotomy, and both hold that necessary truths cannot be validated by experience. The difference is only this: for the traditional philosophers, necessity is a metaphysical phenomenon, grasped by an act of intuition; for the conventionalists, it is a product of man's subjective choices. The relationship between the two viewpoints is similar to the relationship between Platonists and nominalists on the issue of essences. In both cases, the moderns adopt the fundamentals of the traditionalist position; their "contribution" is merely to interpret that position in an avowedly subjectivist manner.

In the present issue, the basic error of both schools is the view that facts, some or all, are contingent. As far as metaphysical reality is concerned (omitting human actions from consideration, for the moment), there are no "facts which happen to be but could have been otherwise" as against "facts which must be." There are only: facts which *are*.

The view that facts are contingent—that the way things actually are is only one among a number of alternative possibilities, that things could have been different metaphysically—represents a failure to grasp the Law of Identity. Since things are what they are, since everything that exists possesses a specific identity, nothing in reality can occur causelessly or by chance. The nature of an entity determines what it can do and, in any given set of circumstances, dictates what it *will* do. The Law of Causality is entailed by the Law of Identity. Entities follow certain laws of action in consequence of their identity, and have no alternative to doing so.

Metaphysically, all facts are inherent in the identities of the entities that exist; i.e., all facts are "necessary." In this sense, to be *is* to be "necessary." The concept of "necessity," in a metaphysical context, is superfluous.

(The problem of epistemology is: how to discover facts, how to discover what *is*. Its task is to formulate the proper methods of induction, the methods of acquiring and validating scientific knowledge. There is no problem of grasping that a fact is necessary, after one has grasped that it is a fact.)

For many centuries, the theory of "contingent facts" was associated with a supernaturalistic metaphysics; such facts, it was said, are the products of a divine creator who could have created them differently—and who can change them at will. This view represents the metaphysics of miracles—the notion that an entity's actions are unrelated to its nature, that anything is possible to an entity regardless of its identity. On this view, an entity acts as it does, not because of its nature, but because of an omnipotent God's decree.

Contemporary advocates of the theory of "contingent facts" hold, in essence, the same metaphysics. They, too, hold that anything is possible to an entity, that its actions are unrelated to its nature, that the universe which exists is only one of a number of "possible worlds." They merely omit God, but they retain the consequences of the religious view. Once more, theirs is a secularized mysticism.

The fundamental error in all such doctrines is the failure to grasp that *existence is a self-sufficient primary*. It is not a product of a supernatural dimension, or of anything else. There is nothing antecedent to existence, nothing apart from it—*and no alternative to it*. Existence exists—and only existence exists. Its existence and its nature are irreducible and unalterable.

The climax of the "miraculous" view of existence is represented by those existentialists who echo Heidegger, demanding: "Why is there any being at all and not rather nothing?"—i.e., why does existence exist? This is the projection of a zero as an alternative to existence, with the demand that one explain why existence exists and not the zero.

Non-existentialist philosophers typically disdain Heidegger's alleged question, writing it off as normal existentialist lunacy. They do not apparently realize that in holding facts to be contingent, they are committing the same error. When they claim that facts could have been otherwise, they are claiming that *existence* could have been otherwise. They scorn the existentialists for projecting an alternative to the *existence* of existence, but spend their time projecting alternatives to the *identity* of existence.

While the existentialists clamor to know why there is something and not nothing, the non-existentialists answer them (by implication): "This is a ridiculous question. Of course, there is something. The real question is: Why is the something what it is, and not something else?"

A major source of confusion, in this issue, is the failure to distinguish *metaphysical* facts from *man-made* facts—i.e., facts which are inherent in the identities of that which exists, from facts which depend upon the exercise of human volition. Because man has free will, no human choice—and no phenomenon which is a product of human choice—is metaphysically necessary. In regard to any man-made fact, it is valid to claim that man *has* chosen thus, but it was not inherent in the nature of existence for him to have done so; he could have chosen otherwise. For instance, the U.S. did not have to consist of 50 states; men could have subdivided the larger ones, or consolidated the smaller ones, etc.

Choice, however, is not chance. Volition is not

an exception to the Law of Causality; it is a type of causation. Further, metaphysical facts are unalterable by man, and limit the alternatives open to his choice. Man can rearrange the materials that exist in reality, but he cannot violate their identity; he cannot escape the laws of nature. "Nature, to be commanded, must be obeyed."

Only in regard to the man-made is it valid to claim: "It happens to be, but it could have been otherwise." Even here, the term "contingent" is highly misleading. Historically, that term has been used to designate a metaphysical category of much wider scope than the realm of human action; and it has always been associated with a metaphysics which, in one form or another, denies the facts of Identity and Causality. The "necessary-contingent" terminology serves only to introduce confusion, and should be abandoned. What is required in this context is the distinction between the "metaphysical" and the "man-made."

The existence of human volition cannot be used to justify the theory that there is a dichotomy of *propositions* or of *truths*. Propositions about metaphysical facts, and propositions about man-made facts, do not have different characteristics *qua propositions*. They differ merely in their subject matter, but then so do the propositions of astronomy and of immunology. Truths about metaphysical and about man-made facts are learned and validated by the same process: by observation; and, *qua truths*, both are equally necessary. Some *facts* are not necessary, but all *truths* are.

Truth is the identification of a fact of reality.

Whether the fact in question is metaphysical or man-made, the fact determines the truth: if the fact exists, there is no alternative in regard to what is true. For instance, the fact that the U.S. has 50 states was not metaphysically necessary—but as long as this is men's choice, the proposition that "The U.S. has 50 states" is necessarily *true*. A true proposition *must* describe the facts as they are. In this sense, a "necessary truth" is a redundancy, and a "contingent truth" a self-contradiction.

Logic and Experience

Throughout its history, philosophy has been torn by the conflict between the rationalists and the empiricists. The former stress the role of logic in man's acquisition of knowledge, while minimizing the role of experience; the latter claim that experience is the source of man's knowledge, while minimizing the role of logic. This split between logic and experience is institutionalized in the theory of the analytic-synthetic dichotomy.

Analytic statements, it is said, are independent of experience; they are "logical" propositions. Synthetic statements, on the other hand, are devoid of logical necessity; they are "empirical" propositions.

Any theory that propounds an opposition between the logical and the empirical, represents a failure to grasp the nature of logic and its role in human cognition. Man's knowledge is not acquired by logic apart from experience or by experience apart from logic, but *by the application of logic to experience*. All truths are the product of a logical identification of the facts of experience.

Man is born *tabula rasa;* all his knowledge is based on and derived from the evidence of his senses. To reach the distinctively human level of cognition, man must conceptualize his perceptual data—and conceptualization is a process which is neither automatic nor infallible. Man needs to discover a method to guide this process, if it is to yield conclusions which correspond to the facts of reality—i.e., which represent knowledge. The principle at the base of the proper method is the fundamental principle of metaphysics: the Law of Identity. In reality, contradictions cannot exist; in a cognitive process, a contradiction is the proof of an error. Hence the method man must follow: to identify the facts he observes, in a non-contradictory manner. This method is logic—"the art of non-contradictory identification." *(Atlas Shrugged.)* Logic must be employed at every step of a man's conceptual development, from the formation of his first concepts to the discovery of the most complex scientific laws and theories. Only when a conclusion is based on a non-contradictory identification and integration of all the evidence available at a given time, can it qualify as knowledge.

The failure to recognize that logic is man's method of cognition, has produced a brood of artificial splits and dichotomies which represent restatements of the analytic-synthetic dichotomy from various aspects. Three in particular are prevalent today: logical truth vs. factual truth; the logically possible vs. the empirically possible; and the a priori vs. the a posteriori.

The logical-factual dichotomy opposes truths which are validated "merely" by the use of logic (the analytic ones), the truths which describe the facts of experience (the synthetic ones). Implicit in this dichotomy is the view that logic is a subjective game, a method of manipulating arbitrary symbols, not a method of acquiring knowledge.

It is the use of logic that enables man to determine what is and what is not a fact. To introduce an opposition between the "logical" and the "factual" is to create a split between consciousness and existence, between truths in accordance with man's method of cognition and truths in accordance with the facts of reality. The result of such a dichotomy is that logic is divorced from reality ("Logical truths are empty and conventional")—and reality becomes unknowable ("Factual truths are contingent and uncertain"). This amounts to the claim that man has no method of cognition, i.e., no way of acquiring knowledge.

The acquisition of knowledge, as Ayn Rand has observed, involves two fundamental questions: "*What* do I know?" and "*How* do I know it?" The advocates of the logical-factual dichotomy tell man, in effect: "You can't know the 'what' —because there is no 'how.' " (These same philosophers claim to know the truth of their position by means of unanswerable logical argument.)

To grasp the nature of their epistemological procedure, consider a mathematician who would claim that there is a dichotomy between two types of truth in the matter of adding columns of figures: truths which state the actual sum of a given column *versus* truths which are reached by adherence to the laws of addition—the "summational truths" vs. the "additive truths." The former represent the actual sums—which, however, are unfortunately unprovable and unknowable, since they cannot be arrived at by the methods of addition; the latter, which are perfectly certain and necessary, are unfortunately a subjective fantasy-creation, with no relationship to actual sums in the actual world. (At this point, a pragmatist mathematician comes along and provides his "solution": "Adding," he tells us, "may be subjective, but it works." Why does it? How does he know it does? What about tomorrow? "Those questions," he replies, "aren't fruitful.")

If mathematicians were to accept this doctrine, the destruction of mathematics would follow. When philosophers accept such a doctrine, the same consequences may be expected—with only this difference: the province of philosophy embraces the total of human knowledge.

Another restatement of the analytic-synthetic dichotomy is the view that opposes the "logically" possible and the "empirically" possible.

If the proposition that a given phenomenon exists is not self-contradictory, then that phenomenon, it is claimed, is "logically" possible; if the proposition *is* self-contradictory, then the phenomenon is "logically" impossible. Certain phenomena, however, although logically possible, are contrary to the "contingent" laws of nature that men discover by experience; these phenomena are "empirically"—but not "logically"—impossible. Thus, a married bachelor is "logically" impossible; but a bachelor who can fly to the moon by means of flapping his arms, is merely "empirically" impossible (i.e., the proposition that such a bachelor exists is not self-contradictory, but such a bachelor is not in accordance with the laws that happen to govern the universe).

The metaphysical basis of this dichotomy is the premise that a violation of the laws of nature would not involve a contradiction. But, as we have seen, the laws of nature are inherent in the identities of the entities that exist. A violation of the laws of nature would require that an entity act in contradiction to its identity; i.e., it would require the existence of a contradiction. To project such a violation is to endorse the "miraculous" view of the universe, as already discussed.

The epistemological basis of this dichotomy is the view that a concept consists only of its definition. According to the dichotomy, it is logically impermissible to contradict the definition of a concept; what one asserts by this means is "logically" impossible. But to contradict any of the *non-defining* characteristics of a concept's referents, is regarded as logically permissible; what one asserts in such a case is merely "empirically" impossible.

Thus, a "married bachelor" contradicts the definition of "bachelor" and hence is regarded as "logically" impossible. But a "bachelor who can fly to the moon by means of flapping his arms" is regarded as "logically" possible, because the *definition* of "bachelor" ("an unmarried man") does not specify his means of locomotion. What is ignored here is the fact that the concept "bachelor" is a subcategory of the concept "man," that as such it includes all the characteristics of the entity "man," and that these exclude the ability to fly by flapping his arms. Only by reducing a concept to its definition and by evading all the other characteristics of its referents can one claim that such projections do not involve a self-contradiction.

Those who attempt to distinguish the "logically" possible and the "empirically" possible commonly maintain that the "logically" impossible is unimaginable or inconceivable, whereas the merely "empirically" impossible is at least imaginable or conceivable, and that this difference supports the distinction. For instance, "ice which is not solid" (a "logical" impossibility) is inconceivable; but "ice which sinks in water" (a merely "empirical" impossibility) is at least conceivable, they claim, even though it does not exist; one need merely visualize a block of ice floating on water, and suddenly plummeting straight to the bottom.

This argument confuses Walt Disney with metaphysics. That a man can project an image or draw an animated cartoon at variance with the facts of reality, does not alter the facts; it does not alter the nature or the potentialities of the entities which exist. An image of ice sinking in water does not alter the nature of ice; it does not constitute evidence that it is possible for ice to sink in water. It is evidence only of man's capacity to engage in fantasy. Fantasy is not a form of cognition.

Further: the fact that man possesses the capacity to fantasize does not mean that the opposite of demonstrated truths is "imaginable" or "conceivable." In a serious, epistemological sense of the word, a man *cannot* conceive the opposite of a proposition he knows to be true (as apart from propositions dealing with man-made facts). If a proposition asserting a metaphysical fact has been demonstrated to be true, this means that that fact has been demonstrated to be inherent in the identities of the entities in question, and that any alternative to it would require the existence of a contradiction. Only ignorance or evasion can enable a man to attempt to project such an alternative. If a man does not know that a certain fact has been demonstrated, he will not know that its denial involves a contradiction. If a man does know it, but evades his knowledge and drops his full cognitive context, there is no limit to what he can pretend to conceive. But what one can project by means of ignorance or evasion, is philosophically irrelevant. It does not constitute a basis for instituting two separate categories of possibility.

There is no distinction between the "logically" and the "empirically" possible (or impossible). All truths, as I have said, are the product of a logical identification of the facts of experience. This applies as much to the identification of possibilities as of actualities.

The same considerations invalidate the dichotomy between the a priori and the a posteriori. According to this variant, certain propositions (the analytic ones) are validated *independently of experience*, simply by an analysis of the definitions of their constituent concepts; these propositions are "a priori." Others (the synthetic ones) are dependent upon experience for their validation; they are "a posteriori."

As we have seen, definitions represent condensations of a wealth of observations, i.e., a wealth of "empirical" knowledge; definitions can be arrived at and validated only on the basis of experience. It is senseless, therefore, to contrast propositions which are true "by definition" and propositions which are true "by experience." If an "empirical" truth is one derived from, and validated by reference to, perceptual observations, then all truths are "empirical." Since truth is the identification of a fact of reality, a "non-empirical truth" would be an identification of a fact of reality which is validated independently of observation of reality. This would imply a theory of innate ideas, or some equally mystical construct.

Those who claim to distinguish a posteriori and a priori propositions commonly maintain that certain truths (the synthetic, factual ones) are *"empirically falsifiable,"* whereas others (the analytic, logical ones) are not. In the former case, it is said, one can specify experiences which, if they occurred, would invalidate the proposition; in the latter, one cannot. For instance, the proposition "Cats give birth only to kittens" is "empirically falsifiable" because one can invent experiences that would refute it, such as the spectacle of tiny elephants emerging from a cat's womb. But the proposition "Cats are animals" is not "empirically falsifiable" because "cat" is *defined* as a species of animal. In the former case, the proposition remains true only as long as experience continues to bear it out; therefore, it depends on experience, i.e., it is a posteriori. In the latter case, the truth of the proposition is immune to any imaginable change in experience and, therefore, is independent of experience, i.e., is a priori.

Observe the inversion propounded by this argument: a proposition can qualify as a *factual, empirical* truth only if man is able to evade the facts of experience and arbitrarily to invent a set of impossible circumstances that contradict these facts; but a truth whose opposite is beyond man's power of invention, is regarded as independent of and irrelevant to the nature of reality, i.e., as an arbitrary product of human "convention."

Such is the unavoidable consequence of the attempt to divorce logic and experience.

As I have said, knowledge cannot be acquired by experience apart from logic, nor by logic apart from experience. Without the use of logic, man has no method of drawing conclusions from his perceptual data; he is confined to range-of-the-moment observations, but any perceptual fantasy that occurs to him qualifies as a future possibility which can invalidate his "empirical" propositions. And without reference to the facts of experience, man has no basis for his "logical" propositions, which become mere arbitrary products of his own invention. Divorced from logic, the arbitrary exercise of the human imagination systematically undercuts the "empirical"; and divorced from the facts of experience, the same imagination arbitrarily creates the "logical."

I challenge anyone to invent a more thorough way of invalidating *all* of human knowledge.

Conclusion

The ultimate result of the theory of the analytic-synthetic dichotomy is the following verdict pronounced on human cognition: if the denial of a proposition is inconceivable, if there is no possibility that any fact of reality can contradict it, i.e., if the proposition represents knowledge which is *certain*, then it does not represent knowledge of reality. In other words: if a proposition cannot be wrong, it cannot be right. A proposition qualifies as factual only when it asserts facts which are still unknown, i.e., only when it represents a hypothesis; should a hypothesis be proved and become a certainty, it ceases to refer to facts and ceases to represent knowledge of reality. If a proposition is conclusively demonstrated—so that to deny it is obviously to endorse a logical contradiction—then, *in virtue of this fact,* the proposition is written off as a product of human convention or arbitrary whim.

This means: *a proposition is regarded as arbitrary precisely because it has been logically proved.* The fact that a proposition cannot be refuted, refutes it (i.e., removes it from reality). A proposition can retain a connection to facts only insofar as it has not been validated by man's method of cognition, i.e., by the use of logic. Thus proof is made the disqualifying element of knowledge, and knowledge is made a function of human ignorance.

This theory represents a total epistemological inversion: it penalizes cognitive success for being success. Just as the altruist mentality penalizes the good for being the good, so the analytic-synthetic mentality penalizes knowledge for being knowledge. Just as, according to altruism, a man is entitled only to what he has not earned, so, according to this theory, a man is entitled to claim as knowledge only what he has not proved. Epistemological humility becomes the prerequisite of cognition: "the meek shall inherit the truth."

The philosopher most responsible for these inversions is Kant. Kant's system secularized the mysticism of the preceding centuries, and thereby gave it a new lease on life in the modern world. In the religious tradition, "necessary" truths were commonly held to be consequences of God's mode of thought. Kant substituted the "innate structure of the human mind" for God, as the source and creator of "necessary" truths (which thus became independent of the facts of reality).

The philosophers of the twentieth century merely drew the final consequences of the Kantian view. If it is man's mode of thought (independent of reality) that creates "necessary" truths, they argued, then these are not fixed or absolute; men have a choice in regard to their modes of thought; what the mind giveth, the mind taketh away. Thus, the contemporary conventionalist viewpoint.

We can know only the "phenomenal," mind-created realm, according to Kant; in regard to reality, knowledge is impossible. We can be certain only within the realm of our own conventions, according to the moderns; in regard to facts, certainty is impossible.

The moderns represent a logical, consistent development from Kant's premises. They represent Kant plus choice—a voluntaristic Kantianism, a whim-worshiping Kantianism. Kant marked the cards and made reason an agent of distortion. The moderns are playing with the same deck; their contribution is to play it deuces wild, besides.

Now observe what is left of philosophy in consequence of this neo-Kantianism.

Metaphysics has been all but obliterated: its most influential opponents have declared that metaphysical statements are neither analytic nor synthetic, and therefore are meaningless.

Ethics has been virtually banished from the province of philosophy: some groups have claimed that ethical statements are neither analytic nor synthetic, but are mere "emotive ejaculations" —and other groups have consigned ethics to the province of the man in the street, claiming that philosophers may analyze the language of ethical statements, but are not competent to prescribe ethical norms.

Politics has been discarded by virtually all philosophic schools: insofar as politics deals with values, it has been relegated to the same status as ethics.

Epistemology, the theory of knowledge, the science that defines the rules by which man is to acquire knowledge of facts, has been disintegrated by the notion that facts are the subject matter of "synthetic," "empirical" propositions and, therefore, are outside the province of philosophy—with the result that the special sciences are now left adrift in a rising tide of irrationalism.

What we are witnessing is the self-liquidation of philosophy.

To regain philosophy's realm, it is necessary to challenge and reject the fundamental premises which are responsible for today's debacle. A major step in that direction is the elimination of the death carrier known as the analytic-synthetic dichotomy.

FOR THE NEW INTELLECTUAL

The Philosophy of Ayn Rand

"Everybody seems to agree that civilization is facing a crisis," writes Ayn Rand. "One of America's tragic errors is that too many of her best minds believe—as they did in the past—that the solution is to turn anti-intellectual. The exact opposite is true. . . . A country without intellectuals is like a body without a head.

"This book is intended for those who wish to assume the responsibility of becoming the new intellectuals. It contains the main philosophical passages from my novels and presents the outline of a new philosophical system."

In challenging the prevalent doctrines of our time, Ayn Rand has aroused violent extremes of admiration and antagonism. *For the New Intellectual* presents the essence of her philosophy. It is required reading, for both her followers and her critics.

Signet J9632—$1.95

THE VIRTUE OF SELFISHNESS:

A New Concept of Egoism

by *Ayn Rand*

Ayn Rand here sets forth the moral principles of Objectivism, the philosophy that holds man's life—the life proper to a rational being—as the standard of moral values and regards altruism as incompatible with man's nature, with the creative requirements of his survival, and with a free society.

Her unique philosophy is the underlying theme of Ayn Rand's famous novels.

(#J9699—$1.95)

ATLAS SHRUGGED
by *Ayn Rand*

Tremendous in scope, breath-taking in its suspense, this is the story of a man who said that he would stop the motor of the world—and did.

Is he a destroyer or a liberator? Why does he have to fight his battle not against his enemies but against those who need him most—including the woman he loves?

Ayn Rand says about this book, "To all the readers who discovered *The Fountainhead* and asked me many questions about the wider application of its ideas, I want to say that I am answering these questions in the present novel, and that *The Fountainhead* was only an overture to *Atlas Shrugged*. I trust that no one will tell me that men such as I write about don't exist. That this book has been written—and published—is my proof that they do."

(#E9135—$3.50)

You can discover the application of Ayn Rand's ideas
to modern events and cultural trends in

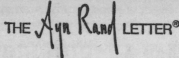

THE *Ayn Rand* LETTER®

Published from 1971 to 1976, the 81 issues of **The Ayn Rand Letter** are
now available, complete and unabridged, in a 400-page bound volume
published by Palo Alto Book Service.

In these essays, Ayn Rand identifies the root causes of recent events,
their ultimate consequences, and the alternative offered by her
philosophy, Objectivism. She writes about a wide range of subjects,
including the energy crisis, inflation, racial quotas, Vietnam, Watergate,
and offers intellectual ammunition for those who seek to understand
and to challenge the dominant trends of our age. $29.95

Also available:

Three lectures by Ayn Rand
Delivered at Boston's Ford Hall Forum
The Moral Factor — 1976
Global Balkanization — 1977
Cultural Update — 1978   Each $1.25

Send your order to:

New American Library, Box 999
Bergenfield, N.J. 07621

Please enclose payment in full. On foreign orders,
adjust for foreign exchange.
This offer is subject to withdrawal without notice.

Order Form

Please send me the following:

The Ayn Rand Letter	@ $29.95	_____
Postage	2.00	_____
The Moral Factor	1.25	_____
Global Balkanization	1.25	_____
Cultural Update	1.25	_____
Postage (lectures only)	.50	_____
Foreign Exchange		_____
	TOTAL $	_____

_____

print name above

_____

address   apt. #

_____

city   state   zip

Please allow at least 6 weeks for delivery.
Price is subject to change without notice.